DAVID BERGER

Creative Jazz
Composing & Arranging II

WRITING
for
SINGERS

Such Sweet Thunder
Such Sweet Thunder Publishing
www.SuchSweetThunderMusic.com

Note to the Reader

Each chapter in this book includes full and partial recordings, an in-depth anlysis, and full scores. While I would have loved to provide everything in one place, the high cost of publishing such a package would have made it impossible for me to produce, and very expensive for you to buy.

In order to make this book affordable and practical, we have put the music videos and scores online. With the scores separate from the text, you can easily go back and forth between them without having to turn pages. Each video also shows coordinated pages from the score that you can follow as you listen.

Each song has two scores, one in landscape format, which you'll see as you play each video, and one as a downloadable pdf, in portrait format with a concert reduction added—all reeds and all brass parts are shown together, in concert key. Each reduction has tags showing the different techniques used.

♪ To download these recordings and scores free of charge, go to:
www.suchsweetthundermusic.com/ pages/cjca2-accompanying-files

All the arrangements in this book are available at SuchSweetThunderMusic.com and all major digital music services.

PERSONNEL ON THE RECORDINGS

Conductor & Arranger: David Berger
Producer: Andy Farber

SESSION A: April 1, 2010 Clinton Studios, NYC
Vocals: Denzal Sinclaire
Reeds: Jay Brandford, Matt Hong, Dan Block, Mark Hynes, Carl Maraghi
Trumpets: Bob Millikan, Brian "Fletch" Pareschi, Irv Grossman, Brandon Lee
Trombones: Wayne Goodman, Ryan Keberle, Clint Sharman
Piano: Isaac ben Ayala
Bass: Yasushi Nakamura
Drums: Jimmy Madison

SESSION B: October 11, 2010 Sear Sound, NYC
Same personnel as above, except:
Vocals: Add Champian Fulton on *All By Myself*
Reeds: Paul Nedzella replaces Maraghi.
Trumpets: Mike Rodriguez and Alex Norris replace Pareschi and Grossman.
Trombones: Marshall Gilkes and Jeff Bush replace Sharman and Keberle.

Creative Jazz Composing & Arranging II:
Writing For Singers
Copyright ©2019 by Such Sweet Thunder Publishing

All the information in this book is published in good faith and for general information purposes only. David Berger and Such Sweet Thunder Publishing do not make any warranties about the completeness, reliability and accuracy of this information.

Any action you take based on the information you find herein is strictly at your own risk. David Berger and Such Sweet Thunder Publishing will not be liable for any losses and/or damages in connection with the use of this book.

If you require any more information or have any questions about this disclaimer, please feel free to contact us by email at:
information@SuchSweetThunderMusic. com.

Book and Cover Design by
Nina Schwartz/Impulse Graphics
ISBN: 978-1-7335931-0-6
First Edition: January 31, 2019

Contents

Scores (Portrait Scores with Concert Reduction)
www.suchsweetthundermusic.com/
pages/**cjca2**-accompanying-files

1. A Perfect Day

2. A Pretty Girl Is Like A Melody

3. All At Sea

4. All By Myself

5. I Was So Young

6. No Sign Of You

7. The Opposite End Of The Bar

8. Smiles

9. Those Lips, Those Eyes

Videos
www.suchsweetthundermusic.com/
pages/**cjca2**-accompanying-files

Song (Recording Session)

1. A Perfect Day (B)

2. A Pretty Girl Is Like A Melody (A)

3. All At Sea (A)

4. All By Myself (B)

5. I Was So Young (B)

6. No Sign Of You (A)

7. The Opposite End Of The Bar (A)

8. Smiles (B)

9. Those Lips, Those Eyes (B)

Dedication

Paul Mendenhall in 2009.

I dedicate this book to my good friend and lyricist, Paul Mendenhall. For eight years we wrote songs and created shows together constantly. It didn't matter whether the music or the lyrics came first. Whatever material we were given by each other excited us no end.

Most of the time we lived on different coasts, 3000 miles apart, and talked nearly daily on the phone deep into the night. When Paul sent me a lyric, I could hear the music even before I finished reading his words. When I sent him a tune at the end of my night in New York, I would wake up the next morning to see his lyric in my email box.

I've never known anyone who loved the American Songbook and Broadway shows more. His knowledge was encyclopedic. I will always be deeply indebted to him for all he taught me and for the great opportunity to hear his words sung to my music.

We loved working together. We weren't afraid to suggest changes, because we trusted each other. Our goal of creating the best songs and shows we could precluded defending our individual egos.

We rarely disagreed, but when we did, we listened to the other side and usually arrived at a third solution, which was even better than either of us would have come to on our own. In his gentle way, he made me into a true collaborator in the spirit of wedding words and music to tell a story, and through it, expressing our deepest selves.

Paul Mendenhall, 1954-2016

Introduction

There is a famous old story about Ben Webster coming to a complete halt in the middle of one of his great tenor saxophone solos. When asked what happened, he said, "I forgot the words." Saxophone great Sonny Rollins insisted on learning the words to every song he played. Frank Sinatra said that when he learned a song, he always learned the words first, before he even sang one note. Do you ever wonder why jazz stopped being popular? One reason may be that we stopped singing, and playing, the words.

When I was in high school and college, I planned on a career as an arranger in New York City. I envisioned spending most of my time writing and recording arrangements for singers with orchestras and bands of various sizes. I also figured that, once in a while, I would get to make an instrumental jazz recording as my reward for all the nice settings I would create for popular singers of mostly standards and show tunes. I had grown up watching Perry Como, Frank Sinatra, Nat Cole, Dinah Shore, Dean Martin, Sammy Davis Jr., and a host of other great singers on TV. Although rock and roll was popular with my contemporaries, adults still loved hearing the standards and show tunes. How was I to know this world was rapidly dying?

So I really didn't expect to have a career in jazz. Much as I loved jazz, I didn't think I could make much of a living at it. Besides, I loved writing for singers! I loved Marty Paich's charts for Sammy Davis, Gil Evans's and Al Cohn's charts for Astrud Gilberto, and especially the first record Thad Jones did with Joe Williams (*Presenting Joe Williams and Thad Jones/Mel Lewis, the Jazz Orchestra,* 1966). When I was at the Eastman School of Music in the summer of 1967, Manny Albam brought Thermofax copies of the scores from Joe's and Thad's record dates to class. I dreamed of writing dates like that for Joe Williams, Sarah Vaughan, Sammy Davis... Well, I never got to write for *them*. But I have gotten to write, and conduct, for many other great singers. So I consider myself very lucky.

I've known pianists who accompanied singers and complained all the while—not me. I have always looked at vocal arrangements as a way to help the singer tell the story—kind of like the contribution sets and costumes give to a show.

When I was playing in Gerry Mulligan's Concert Jazz Band, at a rehearsal we played Bob

Frank Sinatra with arranger Axel Stordahl at Liederkrantz Hall, New York, 1947. Photo by William Gottlieb. Source: Library of Congress.

Brookmeyer's chart of *Bweebida Bobbida*. During the next break I told Bob that I was surprised at how dissonant the voicings were. Although I had listened to the recording hundreds of times, I had never noticed all the half steps and major 7ths inside the voicings. He told me that he had learned to hide the dissonances during his days writing commercial music.

When writing for singers I don't want to dumb down the music, and yet I don't want to upstage the singer. The relationship between the band and the singer must be symbiotic. You've got to know the strengths and weaknesses, as well as the personality, of your singer. I wrote completely differently for Jon Hendricks than I did for Mary Martin. I knew both their styles well, and also what they liked and were looking for. Then I found a way to have fun with both.

Back in the 1970s, when I was playing trumpet with Lee Konitz's Nonet, Bill Rowen came to one of our gigs accompanied by one of my favorite arrangers, Bob Freedman. Although Bill had copied for both of us for years, Bob and I had never met. Bill introduced us, whereupon I proceeded to tell Bob how much I loved his arrangements. He didn't believe that I knew his work, so I proved it by citing, among others, two vocal charts he had ghosted for Thad Jones (*Night Time Is The Right Time* and *Black Coffee*). I then asked if I could take a lesson from him. After a while, we agreed that I would hang out with him for an afternoon.

And so, I went to his apartment. It was very neat and spare. I asked what he was working on. He said that he was arranging a show for Ethel Merman at Radio City Music Hall, to which I asked, "What do you do for Ethel Merman?" She seemed so over-the-top corny to

Ethel Merman in 1967. Source: ABC Television via Wikipedia.

me. This was late in her career, and, like many singers, she had become a caricature of herself. Bob said, "I'll tell you what I *don't* do—I don't try to teach her music." That was one of the best lessons I ever got.

The business of writing for singers is tricky. You don't want to overpower them or betray the meaning of the words. On the other hand, you don't want to be so bland that you don't make the song come alive. I'll be honest—I've made both mistakes—fortunately, not too often. If I'm conducting or attending the first rehearsal or recording, I can make adjustments in the arrangement if need be. I try to get it right, so the chart will read down, but sometimes it just needs a little tweaking. Sometimes a chart sounds good right away, but then I may get an idea to build on it a bit. I'm always sensitive to what the performers bring to the music. They may open a door I didn't see.

Like most arrangers, I'm not too crazy about being told to change what I've written—but that is part of the game. Singers, bandleaders, musical directors, directors, choreographers and producers may all have their own ideas. It's then my job to give them what they want, and make it fit my aesthetic. This usually happens on the fly. I've learned to think on my feet. Fortunately for me, this doesn't happen too often, and, if it does, it's usually something minor. Sometimes they are right. I try to be open to that.

Many years ago I wrote a large studio orchestra chart for Susannah McCorkle for a TV show. The song was Alec Wilder's *I Like It Here*, which is a very vanilla, happy, pleasant little song. I thought I'd play it against type and give it a dark Gil Evans-ish treatment. Ray Wright was conducting, and the orchestra read it down beautifully. I thought it was great. Ray thought it was great. Susannah didn't like it at all. She wanted vanilla, happy, etc. Although I disagreed, I kept it to myself and had all the instruments playing the dissonant notes *tacet* their parts. To me it was as if Hamlet had come home and told his mom,

"Congratulations on your wedding. Too bad about Dad. I hope you and Uncle Claude will be very happy."
(CURTAIN)

No drama, right? Oh, well. Half of being an arranger is keeping everyone happy.

In this book we will look at songwriting. as well as arranging and orchestrating settings for songs. I'm not a lyricist (and I don't play a lyricist on TV), but I've worked with some great ones. I'll discuss various methods of collaborating as well as construction, word painting, and story telling.

Not long before he died, I asked my good friend and lyricist Paul Mendenhall, to express things that could be helpful to us composers and arrangers. Here's what he had to say:

What Lyricists Want

"From a lyricist's point of view, the first requirement of a musical arrangement is that the words be intelligible. This may seem self-evident, but take a listen to most popular songs today. How many of the words can you understand? Are you sure? As someone who has spent years not only singing the wrong words to various pop tunes, but even getting the titles wrong, trust me when I say you are probably mistaken in what you think the song is saying. There are several reasons for this.

The main reason is changing technology. Before amplification, singers had only their own voices and whatever acoustics they were dealing with to help them get the words across. This forced them to project and enunciate clearly—both nearly lost arts today.

I think of this quality as 'transparency.' And it isn't only singers who have lost it. The sound engineer's ability to simply raise or lower the volume on various sections of a band or orchestra, chips away at the many ways in which that band or orchestra support the singer. Nowadays, you are all too often confronted with an impenetrable wall of sound that competes with, and often defeats, the singer.

Another reason is the rise of rock in the 1950s and '60s as the dominant popular music. It was the essence of rock to be rebellious in its attitude toward the accepted cultural norms—including literate, sophisticated lyrics. Of course, by now, rock has been the music of the establishment for decades, so such contempt for good writing is nothing more than an affectation.

Nevertheless, it remains. Many rock music critics deride any song with intelligent, well-structured lyrics. That being the case, why would any arranger of new pop material be motivated to help the lyrics along? If the words are bad, better to let them sink into a morass of sound than risk anyone realizing how bad they are! (Not that it would much matter if they did hear the words. I was once discussing a band with someone and mentioned that I didn't like their lyrics. He said: 'Oh, I never pay attention to the words.' 'You've been singing them for five minutes!' I pointed out. 'Really?' he answered. So there you are.)

Paul continues: As someone who aspires to meet the standards of great wordsmiths of the past, I find this unfortunate, to put it mildly. But there is a glimmer of hope. Lately there's been a resurgence of interest in the Great American Songbook. Ears and minds grown slack from a diet of clichés, vulgarity and stupidity, are rediscovering the pleasure and stimulation to be found in songs of style, grace, charm, wit and craft. They are finding that the tried-and-true rules of traditional songwriting, far from being stultifying, are actually liberating. Limitations are the friends of art.

Limits That Help the Songwriter

This may require some explanation. Say that I am writing a lyric to a sentimental Italian-sounding tune. I don't want to fill it with Italian words, one, because I'm American, and two, because those foreign words would then have to be rhymed. They either must rhyme with other Italian words, or with English words that are certain to sound affected and silly. That might work in a song that is light-hearted and fun, like *That's Amore*. But this isn't that kind of song. So the words must *evoke* Italy without using Italian—that is one limitation.

I'm also limited by the number of notes in each line, which establishes the number of syllables as well. One big improvement that Golden Age lyricists made was to eliminate *melisma*, the stretching of one word over two or more notes (although, regrettably, it has returned with a vengeance in modern pop.)

A third limitation—each syllable must be stressed as it would be in normal speech. No em-***pha***-sis on the wrong syll-***a***-ble!

Fourth—the rhymes must be true rhymes. None of that assonance, "eye rhymes," near rhymes, and other slop so endemic in today's pop, that grate on the ear of anyone who knows better.

Fifth—sentimentality, clichés, trite turns of phrase, and so on must be avoided, while still conveying a sentiment that most listeners will relate to.

I could go on, but you get the point: writing lyrics correctly is an activity hemmed in on all sides by limitations. This can be extremely frustrating—so much so that one lyricist has called it 'as much fun as doing one's own root-canal.' And yet those very limitations are a songwriter's best allies.

There is nothing more intimidating than a blank sheet of paper. Where to begin? When the possibilities are endless, you flounder. But when 99% of your options are gone from the start, it is far easier. And paradoxically, it leads to creative avenues you might never have considered. I have sometimes been asked: 'Whatever made you think of *that?*' in reference to some line the listener admired. If I am being honest, I must shrug and admit: 'I was just looking for a rhyme.'

Good lyrical technique makes things much easier for the arranger. Words that sit properly on the music and rhyme correctly, are far easier for the listener to catch. They work hand in hand with the music, rather than at war with it. This in turn helps the arranger, who doesn't need to strive as hard to make the words intelligible.

Of course, the arranger needs to do more than just allow the words to be heard. For the best singers and instrumentalists, the words are paramount. This should be so for the arranger as well. An artful arrangement will support and even develop the lyric, adding layers of meaning and emotion. In some cases, it can even be effective to *subvert* the lyric, working at cross-purposes to achieve a particular effect, like humor or sarcasm. The lyric might be saying one thing, while the music is telling us something else. This is most likely to occur in a dramatic context, where the subtext is of great importance. (For grand examples of this, listen to Jonathan Tunick's orchestrations of Stephen Sondheim's scores.)"

All the elements of a song place limitations on each other, and in the process, reveal creative opportunities.

As you can imagine from what Paul had to say, working with an artistic, articulate lyricist who knows the territory can be most helpful to any arranger and/or composer.

It's always struck me that the three greatest arrangers in jazz were pianists (Ellington, Strayhorn and Gil Evans), and that many of the worst arrangers were also pianists (including many singers' accompanists). Although pianists generally have more harmonic skills than other instrumentalists, they rarely understand that the 4th Tenor is not their left ring finger.

Hopefully this book will be helpful to accompanists in understanding horns; to jazz arrangers in learning how to make singers sound good without sacrificing their integrity, and to anyone else who enjoys playing or just listening to songs.

If you haven't yet read Volume 1 of this series— *Creative Jazz Composing & Arranging*—it may be a good idea to read it first, before you read this book. All the principles it explores for writing instrumental music apply here as well. The history of music (and especially jazz) shows us that the instrumentalists copied the vocalists in order to sound more human, and the vocalists then copied the instrumentalists in order to sound more sophisticated.

Throughout my career I have encountered instrumentalists who resented having to work with singers. Over the course of my 50 years in the music business, I have suffered my share of talentless and unskilled singers. But I have been repaid many times over when Jon Hendricks, Cécile McLorin Salvant, Kathleen Battle, Milt Grayson, Priscilla Baskerville and the scores of other wonderful singers I've been honored to work with, have opened their mouths and uttered the first word at letter **A**.

David Berger
December 31, 2018

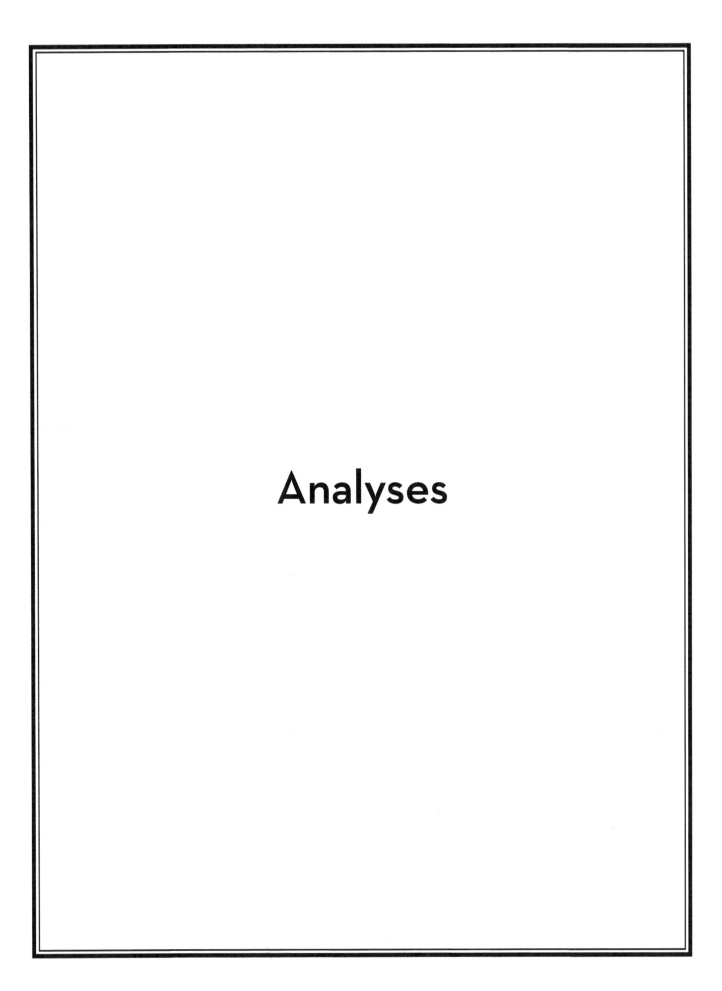

Analyses

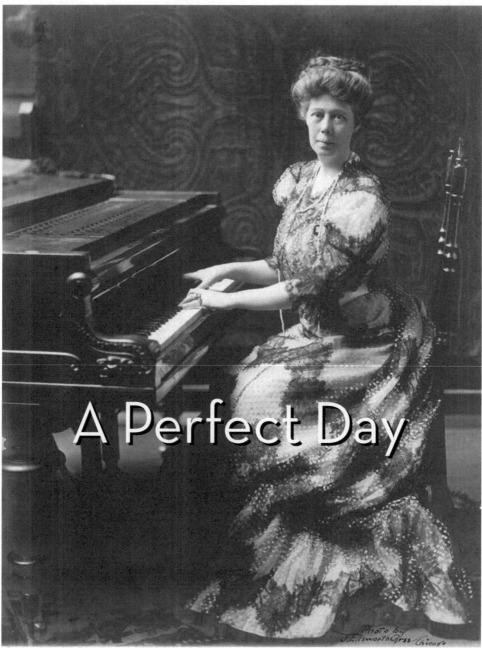

A Perfect Day

Carrie Jacobs-Bond, circa 1910 by J. Ellsworth Gross. Public domain, courtesy of GazetteXtra.

1. A Perfect Day

[At www.suchsweetthundermusic.com/pages/cjca2-accompanying-files, listen to **1-1: Complete Arrangement.**]

One afternoon some years ago, while eating my lunch, I came across a movie from 1939, *Remember The Night,* starring Barbara Stanwyck and Fred MacMurray (five years before they co-starred in *Double Indemnity*). The screenplay was written by the zany Preston Sturges, but it wasn't one of his usual screwball comedies. I was intrigued, to say the least. The movie turned out to be a sweet romantic comedy:

New York assistant district attorney Mac-Murray feels sorry for accused shoplifter Stanwyck, and arranges to get her out on bail for Christmas, ultimately bringing her home to his mother's (Beulah Bondi's) farmhouse in Indiana.

That evening in the living room, after Mac-Murray struggles through *Swanee River* on the piano, Stanwyck says that she can play (having worked in a music store)—whereupon farmhand Willie, played by the soulful Sterling Holloway (whom future generations would know as the voice of Winnie the Pooh) says to Stanwyck and Bondi:

SH: I can sing *The End Of A Perfect Day.*
BB: (discouraging him): Willie...
SH Well, I can.
BB: Well, so can everybody else.
BS: (pulling him toward piano) C'mon, Willie, sing!

Stanwyck accompanies Holloway with the others joining in later. It's just one short understated chorus, but that is the turning point of the whole movie. Stanwyck turns from her life of crime, and through the power of this song, feels the love in this family and finds her true self. I know it sounds corny when I tell it, but the combination of the music, words and the heartfelt vocal performance are one of the best examples of the power of song ever caught on film. Don't expect Pavarotti. It's not about technique or classical tone. It's beyond music. See for yourself: On YouTube, look up *Remember The Night, A Perfect Day.*

After the movie was over, I searched the song, and found the above clip. There's also an article about the songwriter on Wikipedia: http://en.wikipedia.org/wiki/Carrie_Jacobs-Bond

Wow! Did you read that last sentence?

"Jacobs-Bond's life and lyrics serve as testimony to her resilience in overcoming hardships such as poverty, her father's early death, her divorce, her second husband's death, and her son's suicide in 1932 while listening to **A Perfect Day** on the phonograph."

So how come I didn't know this song? Why had it died out with my parents' generation? Too sentimental? How can that be? Pop ballads and Broadway ballads of the past 40 years are way more sentimental. I can't explain it, but this song touched me—the lyric as well as the music.

Here's what Paul has to say:

"Popular songs of this era were usually sentimental, often nauseatingly so, at least from our perspective. They also tended to be *poetic* in the worst sense of the word; filled with trite, flowery images and syntax that was tortured to accommodate a rhyme. **A Perfect Day** is easily identified as of that time; the sunset imagery, the sentiments, the word inversions. What sets it apart is the extent to which this lyric transcends those pitfalls.

First, there is only one inversion that stands out glaringly: 'carol gay.' No one would ever say that; they would say 'gay carol.' But this kind of thing was acceptable in poetry and lyrics at that time. The fact that Jacobs-Bond only indulged in it once, says something for her forward-looking taste. Within twenty years, demotic lyrics—that is, lyrics that sound like real speech—had swept away that kind of thing entirely, except in mockery. Comden and Green loved to spoof this stuff. For example: 'When I was three, my brother stole my lollipop. My lollipop stol-ed he!'

There is also the use of the word 'thought' when one would certainly say 'thoughts.' It's necessary for the rhyme and to eliminate a sibilant *s* at the end of a line—but that is a minor, forgivable lapse.

Second, the sunset metaphor isn't hammered to death, but used more as a mood-setter.

Third, friendship itself is a rather fresh topic. Sentimental songs of the day tended to focus on parent/child relationships or romantic ones. The choice of friendship, particularly new friendship, as a theme, prevents the song from getting too soupy.

Modern songwriters—at least those who know what they are doing—would object to the way the lyric sits on the melody in places. The jump to a high note on unimportant words

like *of* and *with* gives them an unjustifiable emphasis.

Stephen Sondheim, for example, refers to his own lyric for *Somewhere* (from **West Side Story***)* as The 'A' Song, because the melody jumps to a much higher note on that word: ('There's AAAA place for us...'). Yes, of course, that should be avoided. But such concerns had not yet entered songwriters' heads at the turn of the 20th century, so it would hardly be fair to criticize Jacobs-Bond for it. I mention it only because it wouldn't fly by today's standards.

A Perfect Day is one of the few pre-1920 lyrics that can still be sung with a straight face, despite its lapses. That is mostly due to the mood of honest sentiment—rather than sentimentality—that the combination of the words and music achieves."

At the time I encountered this song, I was recording tracks of public domain songs and my originals, with Denzal Sinclaire singing with my big band. In much the same way as I ended the CD I had made with Champian Fulton—one chorus of a slow ballad sung with just piano accompaniment—we recorded this song with Denzal and Isaac. I thought it would make a touching close to a CD.

I gave Denzal and pianist Isaac ben Ayala just a lead sheet with the melody, words, and chord symbols. I had done some re-harmonization to enhance the sentiment of the song, so that it would feel personal to me (and hopefully to our audience). First here is the lead sheet from a fake book *(Example 1-1)*.

Melodic Analysis

We have a simple 16-measure ***aaba*** song form with four 4-bar phrases. The first two phrases

4

LEAD SHEET

A PERFECT DAY

Carrie Jacobs-Bond

Example 1-1: Conventional lead sheet.

start and end on *sol* (the dominant). The third phrase starts on *sol* and ends on *re*. The fourth phrase starts out like the first, but then changes course, so that it ends up in the traditional way—on *do* (the tonic).

A general "rule" of songwriting is that the highest note of the song should appear more than halfway through the song, and should only appear once. Let's call it the "peak note rule." Clearly that doesn't happen here. The *tessitura* of this song is C going up to B♭, a minor 7th. Songs that span an octave or less are easily sung by amateurs, which may, in part, account for the extreme popularity of

A Perfect Day. Large intervals (more than a 5th) can present problems for non-singers. On the other hand, large intervals are what give songs character. Think of Duke Ellington's *I Got It Bad*—"Never treats me sweet and gentle..." "Treats" is reached by an upward leap of a major 9th.

In **A Perfect Day**, the high note (B♭) occurs in measures **1**, **5**, **9** and **13** (the first measure of each phrase). So why does this song work? Not only does the highest note appear at the beginning of the song, but it is repeated three times.

Look at measure **1**. We jump up a minor 6th from D up to B♭. The same thing happens in bars **5** and **13**, but in measure **9**, we leap directly from the C up a minor 7th to the B♭. The omission of the D in this phrase makes the B♭ feel higher, even though it's the same B♭. So we can say that in some cases, the "peak note rule" can be amended to include the "widest interval rule".

Another beautiful touch in measure **9** is sounding the B♭ three beats earlier than in the other phrases. This also draws attention to it in addition to the wider leap up to the B♭.

I'm not big on rules. Principles, yes, rules, no. Let's just say that in many successful songs the peak note appears only once, and that occurrence is about 2/3 to 3/4 of the way through the song.

Chromaticism

There's not a lot of chromaticism in this song, but all five of the accidentals are blue notes. D# and G# translate to E♭ and A♭ enharmonically (the ♭7 and ♭3 in the key of F). The remaining blue note (B♮—the ♭5 enharmonically respelled) occurs in the harmony (the 3rd of G7 and the flat 5th in the F°).

The Original Harmonies

The original harmonies are basically *I, IV, V* with a few little embellishments and detours:

Secondary dominants in measures **2**, **7**, **11**, and **15**.

Passing diminished chords (creating a chromatically ascending bass line) in measures **4**, **6**, and **14**.

Tonic diminished in bar **10**.

My Version

Now, here is the lead sheet that I gave Denzal and Isaac (*Example 1-2*).

Rhythm and Orchestration

As you can see, I kept most of the essential information—all the words and melody notes. For starters I relaxed the dotted 8th rhythms and let the entire song be done freely out of tempo, to make it more like speaking. This gives the performance more emotional impact. I purposely limited the orchestration to piano and voice (no drums, guitar, horns, etc.) Intimacy is primary—the fewer people, the better.

Harmonic Sophistication

In dressing up this song I was very careful to keep in the feeling and sentiment of the original. Very often modern jazz musicians reharmonize standards with chords that don't respect the nature of the melody and words, making the new harmonies feel forced and unnatural. This is certainly not my intent. I aim to flesh out the character of the song. At no time do I want it to sound like a science experiment. Here is the key:

The harmonies should never draw attention away from the story. They should enhance the depth of meaning of the words.

I've pretty much kept all the tonics, subdominants and dominants in place. At least that is where I started. Sometimes I use inversions to smooth out the bass line. One glaring exception is the inserted deceptive D♭7 in the final measure. This "shoulder chord" (♭*VI* with a minor 7th) is a total surprise and begs for resolution to the tonic.

A long time ago, Bob Brookmeyer told me that his overriding concern was tension and release. This is a large part of drama. I choose these points very carefully. Sometimes they are obvious, and much like everyone else's in-

Vocal/Piano

A PERFECT DAY

Carrie Jacobs-Bond
arranged by David Berger

Example 1-2:A My lead sheet..

7

terpretation. Sometimes I delay the release to create a little more drama.

Notating Tensions (upper partials of chords)

I normally don't indicate most chordal tensions, leaving 9ths, 11ths, 13ths and their alterations up to the players. But when I do indicate them, I really need those specific pitches.

Highlighting Peak Notes

The peak notes of phrases are special. It's effective to give them a special harmony that draws the listener's attention to them. In bar **1**, rather than staying on the *IV* chord (B♭), I use a borrowed *ivm* (B♭m) for the B♭ peak melody note. This adds emotional depth to that note (it's the chord of despair). The same situation occurs in measure **5**.

When it comes up again in bar **13**, the harmonic situation is different because, instead of resolving to the tonic in the next bar as before, we are going to a G7-5, so I use a minor *ii V* to the G7-5 as if we were going to Gm—so that we are surprised by the B♮, the major 3rd of the G7. Also notice that the Am7-5 is preceded by its dominant (E7).

The other B♭ peak note, which occurs in measure **9**, is given a Gm7, which then resolves to the original C7. This delays the dominant and gives us a bit of suspense. The Gm7 is set up by a leading tone diminished (F#°). This relieves the stasis of C7 (especially since the melody goes to repeated C's—it's much more interesting and dramatic *not* to have the melody and bass agree).

A minor peak note is the G in measure **3**. The B° is especially attractive here for two reasons: it creates an upwardly chromatic bass

line, and the G forms a major 7th interval with the A♭ (the diminished 7th of the chord) before resolving to the chord tone F (the flat 5th of B°).

Other Passing Chords

Aside from the diminished sandwich chords, I have added a liberal peppering of colorful passing chords. Here is a measure-by-measure account:

Bar 1. B♭maj7 resolving to B♭m6 (*IV* to *ivm*).

Bar 2. Diatonic progression *I ii7*; the Gm7 is both a *ii* in F major and a *vi* in B♭ major. It then proceeds to the *ii V* in B♭ (Cm7 F7). I've added a -9 on the F7 to give it more sentimentality.

Bar 3. B° passing diminished.

Bar 4. Descending diatonic bass line and chord progression (*I*⁶/4 *IV iii ii*—which resolves down a step to the tonic in the next measure).

Bar 5. Leading tone dominant (A7+9) resolves chromatically upward. ivm on 4th beat, which resolves up a step to the second inversion tonic on the next measure.

Bar 6. Passing diminished, then Dm Dm/C, chromatic descending bass line down to A. The Bm7-5 is a *ii* in Am, the E♭7 is a tritone sub of A7 (the *V* of D7). However, the B♭ in the bass leads to the A, which is the 5th on the bottom of the D7.

Bar 7. The secondary dominants moving around the cycle of 5ths is interesting enough, especially since the first note is the 9th of D7.

Bar 8. Gm7 is an *appoggiatura* chord to the C7, delaying the resolution of the F to the E. The F#° is *vii*° leading to Gm7.

Bar 9. Again Gm7 is an appoggiatura chord to C7. The -9 on the C7 adds sentimentality to the word "end."

Bar 10. Instead of the tonic diminished to harmonize the G#, I used an Emaj7 resolving to an F6. All the voices move up chromatically, except the D#, which moves down chromatically to the D of the F6. The D7+9 gives us movement on the second half of the bar and creates some needed tension. (Sitting on an F6 feels too static and plain.)

Bar 11. Rather than sit on G7 for the whole bar, I approach the Db7 in bar **12** with its dominant (Ab7), preceeded by Dm7, which is the ii in C. We expect that to resolve to a G7. The Db7 replaces the G7, and the Ab7 is inserted between them. The A7 on beat 2 is the dominant of Dm.

I also considered using a Bb7 on the downbeat of bar **11** in place of the G7. The melody would be the flat 5th, which I like, and the chord would resolve down by half step to A7, which I also like. But I'm not all that thrilled with the completely parallel chords here. I think the G13 to A7 is stronger.

Bar 12. The Db7-5 resolves down by half-step to the C7. It delays the resolution to the dominant. Since the melody is G, the 5th of the dominant (C7), it would be nice to get a more interesting melody/bass relationship before resolving to the dominant. This exact situation (5th of the dominant in the melody) comes up a lot of times. This is a common solution.

Bar 14. Let's skip bar **13** for a second. Rather than repeat the tonic in bar **14**, as I did in measures **2** and **6**, I used the *V/V* with a -5 with thanks to Billy Strayhorn—*Take The A Train*. This is a surprise and helps to make the ending of the song special.

Bar 13. Working backwards from bar **14**, the D7+9 is the dominant of G7. I like the +9 here because it makes a 4th interval with the Bb in the melody (a peak note). The Am7-5 is the *ii* of Gm, which then resolves to the D7 (V of Gm), the following G7-5 has a surprise B♮ and C#.

The E7 on the second beat is the dominant of A (the root of Am7-5). Notice also that the F on the downbeat resolves down a half step to the E7. We've had so many upward chromatic resolutions in this song that it is refreshing to hear the opposite, the more common downward resolution.

Bar 15. This is an unusual move: substituting a secondary dominant with a diatonic chord. We normally do the opposite. For instance instead of Gm7, we often will use a G7. In this measure the original chord is G7 *(V/V)*, but since I used that chord in the previous measure, I need some movement towards the dominant, and the ii7 works nicely. On the 3rd beat, I put a C in the bass to create a dominant sus4 chord and then when the melody resolves to the E, I harmonize that with an altered dominant.

Bar 16. The "shoulder chord" (Db7) is a nice touch here. It's perfect for the sentiment of the song. This chord can be overused. I recommend saving it for when it's the perfect situation.

Performance

Although I could have easily written out a piano part, I opted to let Isaac improvise his own part, including creating an introduction and ending. He's a most creative pianist, and I knew he would enjoy having more interaction with Denzal.

We recorded this song at the end of a big band session. Denzal and Isaac took a short break while the other musicians packed up and left the studio. Then we set up a microphone for Denzal next to the piano. I gave them an idea of the pace, and encouraged them to be conversational and let the time feeling be luxurious. I think we did eight takes. Each was quite good, but each successive one got more relaxed. This was a clear example of knowing your performers and giving them just enough information to inspire them to create.

Incidentally, you will notice that Isaac doesn't play all my chord changes. This varied from take to take. It's important to me that the performers play and sing what is comfortable for them. The goal is for them to always sound like they are making up the music as they go along, while, paradoxically, the music is so well structured that it must have been thought out.

[At www.suchsweetthundermusic.com/pages/ cjca2-accompanying-files, listen again to **1-1: Complete Arrangement.**] Does this recording feel relevant or merely like an ancient curio?]

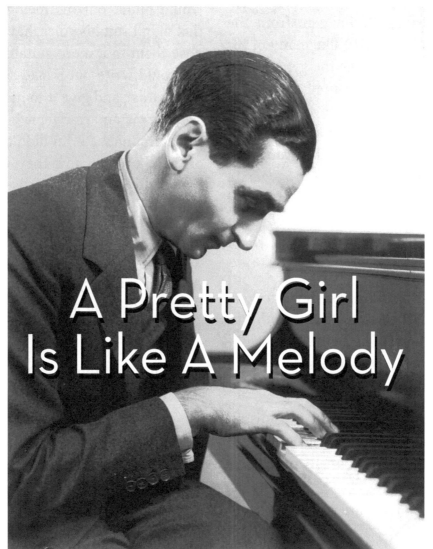

A Pretty Girl
Is Like A Melody

Irving Berlin in 1937. NBC Radio-photo by Ray Lee Jackson. Public domain via Wikipedia.

2. A Pretty Girl Is Like A Melody

[At www.suchsweetthundermusic.com/pages/cjca2-accompanying-files listen to **2-1: Complete Arrangement**.]

This early Irving Berlin gem from the *Ziegfeld Follies of 1919*, like many of his songs, was so popular for generations that we often take it for granted and forget how great it is. Berlin so captures the American spirit. He was and remains the everyman—even after his extreme fame and fortune. His career stretched from 1907-1962 (55 years!). Although he lived another 27 years (he died at the age of 101), by 1962 he felt out of touch with the pulse and taste of Americans, so he retired.

(I find this interesting. Ellington never retired, even though his last hit song, *Satin Doll,* was written 22 years before his death. Many consider the work of his later years among his best.)

On its face, **A Pretty Girl** can be dismissed as a trifle to be sung at beauty pageants. Let's take a closer look. As with so many of Berlin's songs:

- The words are simple, direct and sweet. They capture the vernacular of the time.

- The melody is extremely singable, and yet interesting and memorable.

- The melody suggests all kinds of beautiful and interesting re-harmonization.

- We are charmed by the story.

- The words and melody are perfectly wedded and inseparable. I can't think of this melody without hearing the words in my head.

Berlin composed at a custom-built piano equipped with transposing levers. He could play in only one key—G♭. Weird, huh? So he would plunk out his melodies in G♭, and if that didn't suit his voice, have the levers transpose them to a more suitable key. After that, he would write out a lead sheet (just melody and words), and give it to his assistant. His assistant was an arranger who would then add the harmonies. Berlin didn't know the names of the chords or how they were constructed. He would just tell his assistant to start playing harmonies. If Berlin didn't think a chord sounded right, he'd ask his assistant to play others, until he heard what he was looking for.

According to legend, this is how he wrote upwards of 1000 songs, possibly as many as 1500. Of course, not all of them became hits or standards, but his catalog is as strong as any of our best songwriters'. No less a person than Jerome Kern said, "Irving Berlin has no *place* in American music.... he *is* American music." Berlin composed 25 songs that reached No. 1 on the pop charts, and 51 that became standards; songs as diverse as *White Christmas, God Bless America, They Say It's Wonderful* and *Cheek To Cheek.* Only Harry Warren composed more hits and standards—but Berlin also wrote the words to his songs, while Warren wrote only the music. The only lyricist who rivals Berlin in terms of hits and standards is Johnny Mercer.

There were rumors that Berlin bought some of his songs. I first heard this from my father when I was growing up, and then again in the 1980s, from my barber. That's right, my barber. At that time I used to get haircuts and shaves from Mr. K., whose barbershop at 104th and Broadway was 100 years old; Mr. K. had already been there 50 years. When he found out that I was a musician, he pointed out the window and said, "You see that bar over there across the street? I used to watch Irving Berlin walk in there to buy songs from a colored man who came down from Harlem."

There have always been stories about songwriters buying songs and putting their names on them—especially white songwriters buying them from black composers like Fats Waller. Nevertheless, even if Berlin bought some—and I don't say he did—his amazing ear and extensive output tell me that the bulk of his songs had to be his. Like other conspiracy theories, I think it's fun to consider, but until I have proof, I'm going to believe the conventional story.

Determining the Key of an Arrangement

The most important factors to consider, when choosing a key for a vocal arrangement, are the range of the singer, and where s/he sounds best for particular words and pitches. Often there are several keys that fall within the singer's range. If this is the case, you want to listen for key words and notes to determine which sound most expressive. Since the singer is the primary focus of the arrangement, the singer's best key gets precedence over instrumental considerations. The instrumental parts can then be constructed to fit the vocal key.

Although the original key of **A Pretty Girl** is G, I wrote my arrangement in D in order to accommodate Denzal's voice.

Because Denzal is a fine musician, who plays piano in addition to singing, I sent him the lead sheets for this recording session and asked

him to tell me what keys were best for him to sing. I've done the same for other singers I've worked with, including Cécile McLorin Salvant and Champian Fulton. I have also worked with singers who had their own accompanists to help them determine keys. This was the case with Milt Grayson.

Occasionally, I will sit at the piano and help the singer find his or her best key. Sometimes I have done this over the phone. In some cases I have written arrangements for singers who have previously recorded a particular song, such as when I arranged *I'm Beginning To See The Light* for Natalie Cole and the Jazz at Lincoln Center Orchestra for the Grammy Awards show. Most times I will use the key of the recording. However if the recording was made much earlier, I may have to lower the key. This happened with Milt Grayson, when dealing with songs he had recorded with Duke Ellington decades before. It also happened with Jon Hendricks as he got older.

Let's look at the melody of **A Pretty Girl** (*Example 2-1*, next page). The form is *aba'b'* with 8 bars per phrase. The glorious climax (C#) comes exactly 3/4 of the way through the song (on the downbeat of the **25**th bar) on the surprisingly dark word, "leave." The entire range of the song is a 10th, which is pretty standard for the American Songbook, and very singable. Don't take my word for it. Sing the melody and words. Isn't it great how the words just roll off the tongue? What could be more natural?

The Central Motif

The opening 4-note motif has a chromatic pick-up and then a leap up of a minor 3rd. It is then repeated a step higher with the leap expanded a step to a 4th. The landing note is

LEAD SHEET

A PRETTY GIRL IS LIKE A MELODY

Irving Berlin

Example 2-1: Conventional lead sheet.

repeated twice for emphasis. The next phase leaps down a minor 3rd before ascending by half step. Instead of continuing up chromatically like the original motif, it again jumps up a minor 3rd and then moves up a half step and another minor 3rd. Already fantastic melody writing—the motif is clear and develops using no extraneous material.

The Opposite Motif

While the opening motif ascends, first chromatically and then by minor 3rd, the *b* section of the song has a severely contrasting motif, which is what makes this song so great. Instead of ascending, bars **9-15** descend from high B (the highest note of the song so far) down to B an octave lower (**Example 2-2**). Rather than chromatic, it is basically diatonic. If we eliminate the auxiliary pitches, we are left with B A G, A G F#, G# F# E D C# C B.

For my version (**next page**), I changed the final four notes so that they descend chromatically, which is the inversion of our central motif (let's call that *motif a,* and call the opposite motif *motif b*). I like this, since it is directly followed by the upwardly chromatic *motif a.*

This helps us to see how the two seemingly opposite motifs are similar. We have the rest of the arrangement to follow through on this premise.

Within that big structure of downward diatonicism, the auxiliary notes set up ascending diatonic runs as well as a chromatic moment and leaps of 5ths, 4ths and 3rds that remind us of *motif a* (**Example 2-3**).

The Return of *motif a* (but it goes somewhere else)

The second half of the song begins just like the first 4 measures. Bar **21** has the same melody as bar **5**, but since the melody changes in bar **22**, the harmonies in bar **21** differ from bar **5**. Where bar **6** is chromatic, bar **22** is diatonic, with an upward leap of a major 6th. This is quite dramatic. This high B is the same as the high B in measure **9**, which is tied for the highest note of the tune so far.

The (Sorta) Return of *motif b*

Bars **25-28** are similar in shape, rhythm and construction to **9-12**, with the significant distinction that its starting note is a step higher.

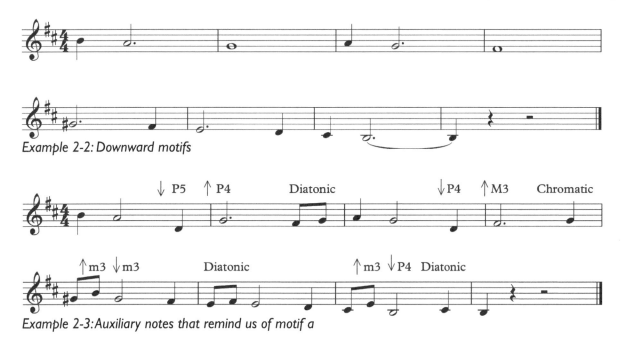

Example 2-2: Downward motifs

Example 2-3: Auxiliary notes that remind us of motif a

LEAD SHEET

A PRETTY GIRL IS LIKE A MELODY

Irving Berlin
arranged by David Berger

Example 2-4: My lead sheet.

The high C# is the peak of the song. It repeats later in that measure, but is unstressed, so its repetition doesn't detract from the impact of the downbeat of **25**. Again we have basic pitches that sequence *sol, fa, mi* in F# major followed by *sol, fa, me* in Em. The chromatic connection in the pick-ups to **25** and the A# to B from **26-27** further develops *motif a*. The final 4 bars are *fa, mi, re, do* in the home key of D with a bit of diatonic embellishment.

My Lead Sheet

My lead sheet (***Example 2-4***) pretty much keeps the same melodic pitches as the original and adds some syncopation to make the rhythms more like how I speak. I didn't expect Denzal to sing the melody exactly as I wrote it. In fact, on this song, and for all the others in this recording session, I encouraged him to be looser in his interpretation—to make it more like the way he would say it.

The Lyrics

I'm not a fan of changing the lyrics of a song. The lyrics and the melody are the two main elements that give a song its character and what make the standards immortal. My only contribution to the lyrics is the tag at the very end of the chart. Here's what Paul has to say about the lyrics:

"Berlin's lyric for **A Pretty Girl Is Like A Melody** is a perfect illustration of how songs changed in the mere ten years after *A Perfect Day* was written. Berlin's lyric establishes a metaphor—a beautiful woman equals an unforgettable tune—and states the argument simply and in a straightforward manner, neither laboring to reach for sentiment nor indulging in pseudo-poetry. Which is not to say it isn't clever. On the contrary, it is far more clever than the kind of lyrics that preceded it. Look at the inner rhymes: 'strain–refrain;' 'upon–marathon.' You will find none of that in the 'thee–foresee' era.

Interestingly, the introductory verse (which is not included in this arrangement) sounds quite old-fashioned: 'an eye for a maid,' 'pretty girlie.' A whiff of lavender perfume seemed to cling to verses, and in time they would be almost entirely dropped. You rarely hear introductory verses today, which is a shame. There is nothing inherently old-fashioned about them, if written with the same care as the main body of a lyric.

Notice also that when the melody jumps up, the pitch that accompanies it always emphasizes a strong word: 'leave,' 'come,' etc. This perfect melding of the tune and the words shows a songwriter at the top of his craft."

Re-harmonization

One of the things that attracted me to this song is its possibility for re-harmonization. My goal is to flesh out the character of the song—to give it more of what it is suggesting. I'm also trying to make it something that I would enjoy hearing and playing. Even though this song is nearly 100 years old, I want it to express how I feel today without destroying its structure and charm.

Melody/Bass Relationship

Step 1 in re-harmonization is to create a bass line that makes the melody sound good and is structurally sound. You must be able to play just the bass and melody and have it sound complete and satisfying. The strongest progressions involve a cycle of fifths or its tritone substitute (sliding down a half step). Every chord in this re-harmonization is one or the other of those two, with the exception of the deceptive cadence (*V7 iii* in the key of G) in bars **9-10**. I could have resolved the D7 to G as in the original sheet music, but the melody/bass unison feels weak to me in this spot. It's best to save that unison for the final cadence in **31**.

Chord Qualities

Step 2 is to determine the qualities and functions, of the chords. Are they dominants, majors, minor 7ths, etc? Usually the melody notes will be the deciders. Where possible I like to use diatonic chords and save the spicier harmonies for when I need something special. Very often the original sheet music will be a good place to start.

For **A Pretty Girl** I'm going to start off with a *V7/V* just as the sheet music does and move directly to the *V7*. The F#m in the sheet music is superfluous. Rather than resolve to the tonic on bar **5**, I'm going to work backwards from measure **9**. Although measure **9** is a *ii V* in G, I'm going to ignore the *ii* (Am7) and precede this measure with the dominant of the *V*. The *V* is D7. The *V* of that is A7. Since the melody in bar **8** is an A, and I don't want the melody and bass to be in unison, I'll use the tritone sub E♭7 (which also moves down chromatically to the D7). It's also tritone-related to the Am7, but we don't really care about that.

Working Backwards

Working backwards from the E♭7, the Em7 is a half step higher than E♭7. I'll use the diatonic *vi7* chord in G, which is also the *ii7* in D. This is a nice pivot chord, since it functions in both keys without altering any pitches. The preceding F7 is the dominant built a half step above the Em7, or you could say that it is the tritone sub of B7, which is the dominant of

Em. F#m7 is a half step above F7 and is the *iii7* in the key of D. The original change there was a tonic D chord, so the F#m7 is a deceptive cadence (*iii* replacing *I*).

The B♭7 in measure **6** is the ♭*VI7* (shoulder chord), which could resolve nicely to a tonic D chord. It also is the V7 of E♭7, which is the last chord in measure **8** (2 bars later). As we saw in the resolution of the E♭7 to the D7 in **8-9**, sometimes chords are inserted to delay resolutions. Note that the melody forms the interesting augmented fifth (enharmonically respelled) above the bass.

Prior to that chord is a B7, which is a dominant a half step higher than the B♭. The 5th is altered in this chord as well, but this time in the opposite direction (flat 5th). The preceding F#m7 is the diatonic chord a 5th above B7, which is the *iii*. The original chord here was a tonic, so again this is a deceptive cadence (the iii chord substituting for the tonic). The melody note, D, is the augmented fifth (again respelled).

The G7 can be viewed as both the subdominant of D with a lowered seventh, and more importantly as the dominant built a half step above F#. The melody note is the flat 5th. I'm very fond of flat 5ths on dominants. They remind me of Thelonious Monk. Also the flat 5th divides the octave in half and creates equal amounts of stability and instability. This is so 20th century—we have the atom bomb to protect us, so we feel safe, but if we use it, and our enemies use theirs, the world will be destroyed. That doesn't make me feel very safe.

Measures **9-10** are essentially *ii V I* in G (the subdominant of D). Since the melody note on the downbeat of **10** is the root of the G chord, I use a deceptive cadence (*iii7*—a Bm7+5). The augmented fifth is the result of the G in the melody. When the melody isn't present (solo choruses, shout choruses, etc.), the simpler G chord is an option.

Bar **11** is the *ii V*, a whole step lower than bar **9**, which makes sense, since the melody is a sequence. We can approach this Gm7 with the *ii V* in G major (Am7 D7) and approach the Am7 with a parallel chord from above (B♭m7). That gives us Bm7, B♭m7 Am7. I remember my teacher, Ray Wright, saying that moving constant structures in parallel motion sounds classy. So our pretty girl is also classy. I like that.

The D♭9 in bar **11** is a common situation. I'm trying to avoid the G melody on a Gm7, so I prepare the C7 with the parallel chord a half step above. Very often dominants are approached from a half step above. That ♭*VI7* can also come where the *V7* is supposed to be and then resolve to the *V7*, thereby delaying the dominant, but that is not the case here.

Bar **12** is *ii V* in E minor (a half step below the previous *ii V*, except this one suggests the minor mode, because E minor is the relative minor of G major). I know that you are thinking, "How can he use F#m7-5 when there is an F# in the melody?" Actually, I use this chord on the solo chorus. When the melody is being sung, I have the bass play these quarter notes: A G# B to avoid the melody/bass unison. To make this sound even more convincing, I have the bass play C, then B♭ on the C7 preceding the A (on the F#m7-5). Stepwise bass lines give a smoothness and logical feel to what may otherwise sound jarring.

Bars **13-16** are basically *V/V* to *V*. This is very common in this spot of *abab'* tunes and also on the last 4 bars of the bridge of *aaba* tunes

(*I Got Rhythm, Honeysuckle Rose,* etc.). Since the melody centers around E (the root of the E7) in bar **14**, I used the tritone sub (B♭7). The break in the bar before the return to the *a* section is also common in many tunes, going as far back as *Tiger Rag.*

The Return of the *a* Section

The first four bars of this song, and bars **17-20** share the same melody and chords. I like to repeat things wherever possible. If repeating doesn't sound good to me, I'll need to develop the material.

Delaying the Resolution

I'm going to stick with the original chord change to start measure **21**. This is the first time in the entire song that we hear the tonic chord. I like delaying the tonic in my harmonizations. Tonics signal agreement (resolution of conflict). It's fun sometimes to delay the resolution until the end of the tune. In this case, the melody is the major 7th on the D chord, so there is still some conflict between the root and the melody.

More Backtracking

Starting on beat 3 of bar **21** up to the downbeat of **25**, I'm going to work backwards. As I learned from the master of harmony, J.S. Bach, you can follow the tonic with any chord and then work your way back to the tonic. It's always fun to go to an outlandish chord. Something distantly related to the tonic. So, don't worry about the continuity, just as long as it sounds good to the ear and finds its way back home.

The original chord change at **25** is C#7, but I'm going to make this *V* into a minor *ii V* (G#m7-5 C#7+9). Now, working backwards from the

G#, I use an A7 (the dominant 7th, built a half step above). That is preceded by *its* dominant, E7. Everything before the E7 moves up by half step (when we are going backwards) and gets as far as A♭7 in measure **21**.

This is very nice on several levels, including the chromatic and cycle-of-fifths root progression, and the chromatically descending 3rds and 7ths from one chord to the next. This is very strong harmony, and will support the tensions in the melody.

Also, nearly every melody note is a tension of the chord: A♭7-5, G13, F#7+5, F9-5, E7 (begins on the 5th but moves to the flat 5th) and A9. I'm attracted to melody/bass relationships where the melody is the 9th, 11th, 13th or an alteration. They sound sophisticated. The caveat is that they must feel natural, not contrived. You never want to lose sight of the story in the song.

25-27 is a chromatic sequence of minor *ii V's* which then resolve to Em. Using *iim7-5* chords avoids the unison melody/bass relationships in the original circle-of-5th dominant chord changes: C#7 F#7 B7 Em. The roots that occur on the 4th beats of bars **25** and **27** are not so crucial, since they fall on weak beats and are of short duration.

The harmonies in **29** and **30** were derived by working backwards from the dominant (A7). These chromatically descending 9th chords work nicely in conjunction with the repeated G's in the melody. Rather than use a turnaround on the melody chorus, I cadenced on the tonic and then did a bit of chromatic planing using major 6th chords.

The Opposites at Work

Have you noticed how much descending chromatic movement there is in this re-har-monization? The motif of the song contains ascending chromatics and the harmonization contains descending chromatics. Ya gotta love the opposites. Even when the melody switches to descending diatonic material, the chromatic harmony reminds us of the original motif. I'm always changing how the opposites are combined. Sometimes they are next to each other, and sometimes one is on top of the other.

[Try playing through the song on a piano or guitar with the original chords and melody, as well as my version. I'm not saying that this is the only way to play this melody or re-harmonize it, but I use this for my arrangement, so it's best to understand it before you go any further.]

The Intro

Whenever I analyze one of my charts, I wonder if I'll be able to explain what I did, because so much of what I do is intuitive. In the case of this chart, my fears were allayed as I analyzed the tune. The intro is a prime example.

The chord progression of the intro comes from bars **1-4**, **13-16** and **17-20** of the tune plus 2 bars of the tonic. The break in measure **6** of the intro is like measure **16** of the tune. The upward half steps in the 1st Trumpet in measures **1** and **3** and the piano/bass figure in measures **5-6** of the intro set up the upwardly chromatic melody in the pickup to **A** (*motif a*). The diatonic descending whole step in the lead trumpet in measure 4 of the intro sets up the descending diatonic *motif b*.

The call-and-response, *tutti* voicings and medium swing complete the picture of this arrangement. This intro is made up of a bunch of clichés but, once the melody starts, we realize that each of those clichés is central to the construction of this piece. In fact you could say that the entire piece is condensed into the introduction.

The *tutti* voicings are simple 4-part close voicings using chromatic approach in the trumpets doubled down the octave in both the bones and saxes. Since there are only three bones for four notes, I left out the third harmony note. The top note will strengthen the lead trumpet and the second and fourth harmony notes contain the 3rd and 7th of each chord. This is a comfortable and immediately identifiable voicing for the bones. The final voicings (measure **4**) are Eb9 to D69.

Note how the chromatics in the horns are reflected in the bass part. Very often I ignore horn passing chords when writing the bass part, in favor of creating a strong melody for the bass. In this case I was able to create a strong melody *and* catch the passing chords.

The Head

My Role as Accompanist

Duke Ellington described his role as creating settings for his soloists. He also said that his goal was to inspire his players to be great. He accomplished both tasks at the piano, as well as with pencil and paper. When I was in school, although I preferred to play trumpet, I was often pressed into service as a pianist. I never had a lot of chops, but I understood harmony and had an intuitive understanding of counterpoint. I could always carry on a musical conversation with both instrumentalists and singers.

I listened to Duke Ellington, Count Basie, Horace Silver and Sonny Clark every day. Although their styles were different, each of them taught me how the piano can make everyone else sound good. I developed a sense of

knowing where the players were going, when they would take a breath, and when they needed inspiration. As an arranger I perform the same function of interacting with soloists and singers, except that I have to imagine what they *might* do, and predetermine the accompaniment. The backgrounds I write for horns are in many cases what I would play on the piano if I were accompanying.

But that is only half of the job. I've got to give everyone in the ensemble an integral part that is perfectly suited to his or her instrument and personality. Years of playing in trumpet sections and small and medium- sized bands gave me firsthand knowledge of the strengths and limitations of all the instruments, and how they sound when combined.

Which comes first, rhythms, melody, harmony, or orchestration? Michel Legrand told the story of being seated next to Igor Stravinsky at a concert. Michel mustered up the courage to speak to one of the handful of great composers of all time. He asked if Stravinsky would mind if he asked him a question. Stravinsky agreed. So Michel asked him what his method of writing music was. Stravinsky thought for a second, and then said, "I sit at the piano, and it just comes to me." I'm sure Stravinsky was being truthful, but that is only half the story, because we know from his manuscripts that after the initial inspiration (that just came to him), he would tinker. That is, he recognized the gift from his subconscious mind and polished it by editing, using his conscious linear thought to perfect the music.

So which does come first, rhythms, melody, harmony, or orchestration? It depends. As I did when I used to accompany on piano, I let my instincts dictate (my subconscious mind where 69 years of hearing and playing music are mixed together with 69 years of living), and then I polish and make sure all four of these elements of music are served. (Actually, at the time of writing this book, I am only 68, but I'm sure I heard my mom play the piano and listen to the radio and records while *in utero*. Music was always, and continues to be, a safe place for me.)

Let's look at the specifics of this arrangement and discuss the techniques and aesthetic issues as they come up in context. No technique is good or bad in itself—but some are more useful and appropriate in certain circumstances than others in helping to tell your story. Context is everything.

Stop Time/Call-and-Response

Often, when tunes start with a break or stop time, I don't use an intro—I'll just start on the head. Here is a case where an intro seemed appropriate and came to me easily. The call-and-response with the voice at letter **A** is given to the three bones in harmony, with the bass doubling the bottom trombone. The bones play the descending chromatic F7 to E7 while the voice holds the D (13th on the F7, resolving by becoming the 7th of E7).

Right away in the first bar, the chromatic nature of the melody, and its inversion in the harmony, are established. The response in bar **A3** is diatonic (Em to A7), but the first trombone moves chromatically down to the -9, so we begin to grasp the complexity of how chromaticism and diatonicism will be dealt with in this chart.

Minor Triad Usage

Note that in **A3**, although I'm implying Em7 to A7-9 (a typical *ii V*, which ordinarily will use a 7th in the Em7 voicing), I have inten-

tionally omitted the 7th in favor of a minor triad. To me the 7th sounds too ordinary and bland. The plain minor triad has a more stark and dramatic personality.

Also, notice that I don't have a 3rd in the A7-9 chord. I suppose that if I had four bones, I might have written D to C#, but then I'm glad I only have three. Adding those extra notes, although they make the voicings more complete, creates less character—the voicings would sound ordinary. Three trombones have a noble sound. Adding a fourth bone tempers them. It removes the bite, and generally makes them too mellow for my taste. Or as Duke Ellington once said, they would be too easy to write for.

Setting Up Early

Very often we like to have the rhythm section set up a bar, two bars, maybe even three bars before a big change is made in the groove. Such is the case in **A4**. The rhythm section starts playing time three beats before **A5**, where the horns catch up. Since the drummer is going to play time on the ride cymbal at **A5**, he should avoid the ride in his pickup. Probably a simple figure on the snare would be nice. I'll leave that up to the drummer.

Word Painting

Here's something I just noticed. I like coloring the words—using the music to give them more meaning. **A5-7** is a good example. "Haunts" gets a mysterious dominant chord with a flat 5th, "you" is neutral, "night" again is mysterious with the dominant flat 5th and "day" is the bland resolution (minor 7th). I mostly do this sort of thing instinctively. For example, if the word "up" is in the lyric, the music generally ascends. But you don't want to overdo this sort of thing. We call that "Mickey Mouse," as in film, where every gesture is reflected in the music. Sometimes it's fun to do the opposite. This can be humorous, or show the complexity of a word or phrase that has both a positive and a negative meaning. I like depth. Gil Evans' music is a great example of this sort of thing. Even his happy arrangements are tinged with sadness. Life is complicated.

Diminution

The call-and-response pattern between the voice and bones in **A1-4** happens twice over four bars. **A5-6** doubles that up, and then there is no response in **A7-8** (leaving space for the rhythm section to respond. Originally I had a sax unison line here but, although it was motivic, it felt cluttered, so I removed it at rehearsal). The first two bone chords continue the same type of voicings as before (root, 3rd, 7th) and then switch to rootless voicings (3rd, 7th, 9th), leaving the roots to the walking bass.

Call-and-Response

B1-3 is a call-and-response between the saxes and bones, with careful attention to good counterpoint with the vocal as well. Good counterpoint means staying away from the vocalist's rhythms and pitches while creating strong melodies that stand on their own. The saxes are voiced in 5-part harmony with a root on the bottom. Actually, the third chord is an A♭9-5 (the tritone sub of D7). I didn't inform the rhythm section; they didn't need to know. The second voicing is a Drop 3 with an added root on the bottom. This change of spacing came about due to the voice leading of the top three voices, and the root and 5th on the bottom.

The bones resume their root/7th/3rd voicings in **B2** and then switch to rootless 3rd/7th/9th voicings in **B3**, much the same as in **A1-5**

and **A6**. However, there are two differences. This time everything is compressed into two measures, and the descending chromatics are increased from two notes to three. It's interesting to hear *motif a* in the bones while the vocal has moved on to *motif b*.

Changing Textures

In **B4** the saxes switch to unison for 3 bars while the trumpets join the bones for a couple of brass hits that answer both the saxes and the vocal. Note the ascending half step/minor 3rd intervals. The brass will pick this up and expand upon it when they switch to unison in **B7**. The brass hits in **B5-6** contain seven different pitches—no doubling here. The first one is a tight cluster, and the second is more expansive, with an upper structure triad and a fall-off. In each of these chords the bones are voiced 1, 5, 7 and the trumpets have the 3rd and the tensions.

The saxes counter with a return to root-anchored voicings that create a pad below the unison line in the brass in **B7**. They are then joined in harmony by the brass for the last two notes, which set up the break. Notice the 1st Alto line for these voicings: up and down a whole step and then down a half step—motifs *a* and *b* are reversed in order and condensed to four notes.

Repeating vs. Creating New Material

Although the words are different, the melody in **C1-4** is identical to **A1-4**. When the opportunity to repeat presents itself, I'll go with that, if repeating feels satisfying. Repetition gives listeners an opportunity to understand the form and understand further what they didn't catch the first time around. Repetition is also great for the band. Change is challenging for players. Players can relax when they have seen something before. If you ever need to write a chart that will read right down, I recommend using a lot of repeated material—especially repeated rhythms.

Measures **C5-6** are identical in rhythm and orchestration to **A5-6**. Only the chord changes, voicings and melodies are different. The unison brass returns in **C7** much as they did in **B7**, ending with two voiced out chords, but this time the saxes are omitted. Although the chord change is an F9, the unison brass ascends a G major scale with an inserted minor 3rd blue note (spelled enharmonically as A#). The 1st Trumpet plays half step, whole, half, half, minor 3rd and jumps up a minor 6th. The half steps and minor 3rd are *motif a* and the whole steps are *motif b*.

What about that minor 6th jump up to the B♭? It's the flat 5th of the voicing and a blue note (♭3 in G, which is the key we are temporarily in). More importantly, the minor 6th interval is the inversion of the minor 3rd interval, but altered by a half step. This may sound like a bit of a stretch, but this is what development is really about: gradually altering the material, so that it evolves in a natural way.

Fresh Colors

Leaving the saxes out of letter **C** makes them sound fresh when they return to play pads at **D**. With the exception of the baritone, which is on the roots, all the saxes are moving in half steps, whole steps, or combinations of the two, before joining in a chromatically descending unison line in **D4**.

By this point, the bones have been out for 4 bars. They return in **D5-6** with the same rhythmic pattern they played in **A5-6** and **C5-6**. This time they play chromatically descending 9th chords voiced 3rd, 7th, 9th. The saxes answer

with a unison ascending half step and minor 3rd before jumping into descending chromatic chords (♭II I). Note the 1st Alto's jump from the unison—up a minor 6th and then down a minor 3rd. I love it when things come back. Who doesn't? This sax figure puts a nice period on the first chorus. Notice that I didn't use a turnaround. I want a full cadence here. The saxes tell us that this section, the vocal melody chorus, is over.

A Confession

This chart was written rather quickly in one sitting. If I recall correctly, it took about six or seven hours, which for me is about average for a chart of this length. It generally takes me about a half hour to write 8 bars. This varies a bit from chart to chart. With the exception of the last 3 bars, I wasn't thinking about the motifs at all. I didn't even analyze the song to discover what the motifs were. I was just responding to the melody, words and harmony in an intuitive way. All this motivic analysis was unknown to me—until I sat down to write this chapter, four years after writing the chart. (That is, it was unknown to me on a conscious level. My *sub*conscious was having a field day.)

So what was my conscious mind doing while I was writing? Good question. I was concerned with editing my first instincts, tidying up rhythms and voicings, thinking about pacing the orchestration, and singing and playing the rhythms to make sure they were swinging and authentic. Judging from the scarcity of erasures on the score, it looks like I didn't change my mind more than two or three times in the whole chart. I originally had trombone solo answers in the intro, and a unison trombone line the first 3 bars of **D**, which I decided were too busy.

Not every chart is so easy for me. Sometimes I get stuck and use my intellect to get my creative subconscious juices flowing. Although I was a pretty good developer, even in high school, I wasn't consistent. Some charts were better than others, and some sections of charts were better than others.

I once heard a similar critique of Lana Turner, a beautiful movie star whose films spanned the late 1930s to the 1960s. She is best known for her role opposite John Garfield in *The Postman Always Rings Twice.* You could taste the animal magnetism between the two of them. According to critics, her problem was that she couldn't sustain this intensity for an entire movie. (Except *Postman.* My guess is that Garfield kept her on her toes. His performance was decidedly underplayed, but at the same time intensely hot. A great script didn't hurt either.)

This same problem of consistency is rampant in jazz composition and arranging. There are plenty of writers with great ideas, but can they tell a compelling story that keeps us riveted from beginning to end? It takes discipline and the courage to be self-critical. By the way, the original title to Billy Strayhorn's masterpiece, *Charpoy,* was *Anal Renrut,* Lana Turner spelled backwards.

Respecting the Song

One of the challenges of writing vocal charts is achieving a balance between the vocalist and the accompanying instruments. The focus must be on the story that the singer is telling. I want all the musicians to have interesting integral parts, but I don't want them to overshadow the singer or distract the listener from the story. In general, less is more. Clark Terry once told me that, after the first rehearsal of a new Strayhorn chart, Billy would casually ask each of the players if he liked his part.

The Egg Test

Another thing to keep in mind is the visual. What is the audience seeing when your chart is performed? When I was in high school I wrote a chart of *When I Fall In Love* for a cute girl, Roberta Murphy, to sing with the big band in our yearly Pop Concert. After the intro, she sang a chorus; then there was a band interlude, after which she sang it out. We read the chart down in rehearsal, and our band director, Herb Schoales, pointed to the interlude and asked me what Roberta was supposed to do while we were playing all this instrumental stuff. His exact words were, "She's standing there with egg on her face." Since that day 50 years ago, I haven't written a vocal chart without giving it the egg test.

Consider the Visual

I believe that one of the reasons why jazz is not more popular is that our performances are not interesting to look at. I get some ribbing for my attention to dress, stage set-up, choreography and staging. I'm well aware that I'm just the music director, but if I can help make a show look better, I'll speak up at production meetings.

I often hear from audience members, "You guys look like you are having a great time." Well, yes, we are. The joy on the bandstand permeates the music and the audience. Just because we are smiling doesn't mean that the music isn't deep. As Morey Amsterdam (in the role of comedy writer Buddy Sorell on *The Dick Van Dyke Show*) so beautifully stated, "Comedy is serious business with me."

Direct Communication with the Audience

How we package our music directly impacts how it is received. Not everyone in the audience is a jazz aficionado. To me, it is just as important to entertain the jazz fan's partner—who may not be all that interested—as it is to entertain the fan, who owns every record that Booker Little ever made. The music speaks for itself, but I can make it user-friendly without diminishing the art. Here are some things I do in performance whenever possible:

1. Have a singer on the gig. Even if he or she only sings a song or two, this will draw in listeners who don't understand instrumental music, and for everyone in the audience, it gives the presentation a greater dimension.

2. No music or lyrics on stage for the singer. He or she must make eye contact while telling the story to the audience. The same should apply for instrumentalists, but it is not always practical. At least soloists should have their music memorized.

3. Jon Hendricks taught me, "Your responsibility as a performer is to dress better than your audience." How you dress shows respect—respect for the music, respect for the other musicians, and respect for the audience. This goes double for singers and dancers.

4. Soloists stand up for their solos. This helps the audience to understand the music by directing their eyes to what is important. If there is a long solo for a brass player, s/he should come down front to play it if possible. The same goes for brass solis. This means the players will need to memorize their parts. Tell the band ahead of time so they can prepare.

5. Talk to the audience; tell them something related to the piece or one of the performers. As conductor, I let the audience in on what we are about. I want to make them feel like insiders. This also fills the dead space while the band is getting up their parts for the next chart. You want the show to flow, so that the energy doesn't dissipate between numbers.

A humorous anecdote is always welcome. Stay away from technical musical jargon—it will only alienate the non-musicians in the audience. The success of a piece has little to do with it having a tone row, tritone subs or great saxophone voicings.

6. Introduce the soloists. Let the audience know how great they are. Duke Ellington was a master at this. He was so gracious. He would say things like, "If you know the saxophone, then you know Johnny Hodges." I never do any name-calling during the music, though. I find it distracting, or, as they say in the theater, "it breaks the fourth wall."

7. When the vocalist is on stage, it is her show. She talks to the audience. The leader introduces her, and while she is on stage, she deals with the audience, and the leader deals with the band. You don't want to mess up her rapport with her audience. She's telling her story.

8. Make sure that everyone, including the vocalist, has eye contact with the conductor. Conversely, effective conducting demands eye contact. Memorize the score as soon as possible so the music is internalized and you can share your joy with the band.

9. When I was first starting out in the business, there was a list of taboos on the bandstand: no white socks, no brown shoes, no smoking, no drinking (of any liquid), no eating, no leg crossing (except the guitarist) and no shaking hands (shaking hands tells the audience that this is a pick-up band and not regular personnel). These things still look unprofessional to me.

My first band was the Jimmy Dorsey Orchestra, which was led for decades by Lee Castle, who had played trumpet with Goodman, Shaw, Tommy Dorsey and a host of other name bands back in the day. I stayed with Lee for nine hilarious months, and then left for what I hoped would be more lucrative and modern work in town.

About six months later, I subbed for my buddy, Danny Hayes, for two weeks with a band at Roseland. It was a grueling job, 40 minutes on, 40 minutes off for 6 hours, 8 times a week—including two matinees.

During one of the matinees, I looked out at the audience. Just outside the dance floor, sitting at a little table by himself, was Lee Castle drinking a cup of coffee and listening to the band, which included several of his alumni. When the set broke, I walked over to Lee to say hi and, before I could get a word out, his eyes gazed down from my smiling face to my brown shoes. I can still hear his raspy voice, "Jeez, Dave, didn't I teach you *anything?*"

10. Present a wide variety of music. Different tempi, grooves, moods, orchestration, keys, soloists, lengths (of pieces and solos), orders of solos, etc.

11. Openers: For over 10 years our band has started just about every gig with *Stompin' On A Riff.* It's a good opener for us because we know it really well and it's easy to warm up on, it's not long, and it's swinging. The piano and then the entire rhythm section set the groove before the horns come in, it builds to a climax and ends dynamically. The audience response is always great. They know there is going to be a lot of swinging in their immediate future. This works for us. Every bandleader or singer needs to find a surefire opener that works every time.

12. Closers: I almost always end sets with an uptempo barn burner. Similarly, we finish nearly every gig with *Jumpin' At The Woodside.* I like to leave people "patting their foot."

[This is a lot to digest. Let's take a listen to **2-2: A-E** and get a feel for how it all fits together.]

Solo Section

Length

This being a vocal chart, I don't want to leave the singer "with egg on his face," so I'll usually keep the solo section short. This usually means just a chorus or even a half-chorus before the vocal re-enters. This can vary, depending on the situation and tempo. When I arranged *They Didn't Believe Me* for Champian Fulton, there were two solo choruses: tenor and trumpet. In the studio while recording the chart, that felt too long, so I penciled in to cut out the second chorus, and had the tenor and trumpet split the 32 bars of one chorus. But when we play the chart live, it seems to need both solo choruses, so I erased the cut. That's why God invented erasers. In general, longer solos tend to work better live than on recordings.

For the most part, on vocal charts, I try not to stay away from the words too long, since the audience is following the story. In the case of **A Pretty Girl**, by the end of Brandon Lee's trumpet chorus, I feel it's time to get back to the vocal. The symmetry of intro, one chorus vocal, one chorus solo, one chorus vocal, and coda, feels right to me.

I once asked Bob Brookmeyer how he felt when the charts he wrote for the Thad Jones/ Mel Lewis Jazz Orchestra were opened up for

10–15 minutes of solos. He said that, although the solos could be exciting, that kind of length obscured the written material and made for an unequal balance in the form of the arrangement. Being an arranger, I naturally agreed with him.

Harmon-Muted Trumpet Solos

Although most jazz musicians and fans associate Harmon mute solos with Miles Davis, there is a tradition on vocal recordings that started with Harry "Sweets" Edison and Joe Newman. They would play behind the singer, a solo between the vocal choruses, or both. This sound was used frequently by arrangers Nelson Riddle, Quincy Jones and Billy Byers in their charts for Frank Sinatra, Nat Cole, Ella Fitzgerald and Rosemary Clooney. Once, when our band was rehearsing for a performance in Paris with Quincy, he wanted some Harmon mute behind the vocalist, so he looked up at Brian and said, "Cootie"—he loved to call Brian "Cootie"—"give me some of that Joe Newman."

Harmon mutes change the sound of the trumpet in three ways: pitch, tone, and volume. Aside from making the horn sound sharp (some brands have better intonation than others), this mute eliminates most of the lows and mid-range sounds, so that the tone produced is piercing and more like a flute or piccolo than a trumpet. Also, the volume is diminished so greatly that solo passages generally need to be miked. When Miles played with a Harmon mute, his mute was touching the mike. Other players have kept a slight distance between the mute and the mike. I encourage you to experiment with one of your trumpet-playing buddies, and hear for yourself.

Although most players nowadays don't use it, the Harmon comes with a stem, which can be removed. When the stem is in, players can create a wah-wah effect by placing their hand over the cup and the end of the stem. The stem can also be left in or extended, and played without the hand over it. This has been uncommon in jazz for the last 50 years, but it can be useful for getting more volume out of the Harmon. The problem is that the stem alters the tone, making it sound more like a straight mute. This is not an issue for the wah-wahs, which sound similar to a plunger/pixie mute combination.

Backgrounds

Although the Harmon is soft, it has a very cutting quality that is not only appealing, but makes it possible to write backgrounds using any and all of the other horns without background and foreground having similar tones. As with any other mute, make sure you give the player at least 4 bars at a medium tempo to insert or remove the Harmon. It might be even better to leave 8 bars on either end of the solo, so that the soloist can walk from the trumpet section (traditionally in the back row of the band set-up) to a microphone in front of the band, and back.

Even with the Harmon's ability to cut through the other sounds, I prefer to keep the backgrounds simple and not loud. In the case of **A Pretty Girl**, I used simple figures and left plenty of space.

Developing a New Idea for Each Chorus

A long time ago I noticed that many of my favorite charts developed one idea for one chorus, a new (but related) idea for the next chorus, and so on. Neal Hefti's *Splanky* is a classic example. The backgrounds for the trumpet solo in **A Pretty Girl** use this technique.

The Charleston

The background to our melody chorus ends with a descending minor 3rd interval in a Charleston rhythm on the first 2 beats of **D8**. I'm going to develop this idea for the backgrounds to the solo chorus (**E** through **H**). Letter **E** starts with a descending 5th in a doubly dotted half note to 8th note rhythm. Both the interval and the rhythm have been expanded, but the shape remains. The same figure happens two bars later with slight alterations in the inner parts to accommodate the change in harmony. In the pursuit of lightness and simplicity, I have voiced these figures in a typical 4-part close harmony *tutti*.

There is a unison quarter note pickup to **E1**. I used unison for that note to keep it unstressed and save the stress for the downbeat voicing at **E1**. **E4** is a displaced Charleston (beginning on beat 3 instead of 1). The mostly chromatically descending voicings are reminiscent of the E♭6 D6 figure in **D8**, only this time the chords are A7+5 G13. Although I've used simple 4-part close voicings for these 4 bars, the melody notes are all tensions, which makes them sound interesting and out of the ordinary.

Thumb Line

The diatonic sax thumb line at **E4-8** creates a sense of calmness and stability after all the turbulent syncopations in the *tutti* passage. They begin with a descending minor 3rd (D to B), which is filled in with a C# between. The descending minor 3rd is followed by ascending 4ths (opposite direction with an expanded interval)—B, E, A. The ascending 4ths idea continues in pairs: E to A and D to G in **E7-8**.

The brass answers the sax unison with offbeat 6-part chords that ascend in 3rds. Notice that the brass voicings are built almost completely in 3rds (1, 3, 5, 7, 9, 11, then 3, 5, 7, 9, +11, 13, etc.). Although stacking 3rds like this may seem like very basic harmony, brass and saxes sound great when voiced this way. The fall-off on the last note before letter **F** helps define the form and smoothly passes the harmonic ball off to the saxes.

5-part Saxophone Voicings

Letter **F** begins with the saxes taking over the role held by the ensemble at **E**. I've kept the rhythm and descending 5th, expanding it to a 6th in **F3**. I've kept tensions in the top voice (9, 11, 9) but then have two chord tones (flat 5th and 3rd) before resolving to the -5 on the B♭9. In order to keep a similarity of tension in the chords, I put the 11th on the bottom of the F#m7-5, so that the bari creates a minor 9th interval with the flat 5th in the 1st Alto. The D# (3rd of the B7-9 chord) has all the saxes in unison—much like the unison pickup to E. With the exception of the F#m7-5 and B7-9, every voicing is 4-part close with the root added on the bottom to create a fifth part. This is simple, but most effective.

Coming to a Semi-cadence

At this point our ears can use a break from the horns. I want to hear the soloist complete the first half of his chorus with just rhythm section accompaniment. Having the horns rest before the next section of a chart is common. Sometimes when we play a repetitive riff, say on a blues, we might play a 2-bar figure five times, and then rest for the last 2 bars of the form.

Repeating Harmonies

When the harmonies repeat, it's often effective to repeat the entire figure or passage verbatim. This happens here—sorta. **G1-3** repeats the *tutti* voicings of **E1-3.** The only difference is in the unison pick-up. Changing the pick-up is just enough to make it feel new, but because everything that follows is the same as before, it feels familiar. The upwardly chromatic pick-ups with the syncopated upward leap are reminiscent of the vocal pick-ups to the beginning of the song when Denzal sings the title words, "A pretty girl." The vocal had a chromatic 3-note pick-up with a leap to the downbeat, and although the shape is the same, the notes have been changed to protect the innocent.

G4 is like **E4**, except that it resolves to the tonic (Dmaj9) rather than the subdominant (G13). What follows is a series of chromatically descending dominants on the *ands* of 2 and 4, finally ending with the rhythm of **G1**. Again note how the lead trumpet has all tensions in this *tutti* passage (+5, 9, 13, -9, 9, 9). All the inside parts move smoothly. Also notice how low the brass is written. I'm not looking for power or brightness. This is a good register for a *mf* background.

Bringing Back Motifs in a Different Place

Remember the 3½ bars of rest at the end of **F**? Letter **H** starts with 3¾ bars rest for the horns. Reversing the order disturbs the predictable symmetry. Next the unison saxes jump up and down a 5th (like the descending 5th in the *tutti* at **E** and **G**) before ascending with our old friend the minor 3rd. While they are doing all this, the trombones play a series of chromatically descending 9th chord pecks reminiscent of what they did in **A5-6**, **B3**, **C5-6** and **E5-6**.

Summing up the motifs gives us a feeling of finality, especially when followed by two measures of rest. While they rest, Brandon

finishes his solo in the clear. Just to make sure that everyone in the band and audience feels the form, I wrote an unmistakable bass line to set up the final chorus. Although this bass line is a well-worn cliché, it is most appropriate here due to our continual use of ascending and descending chromatic lines. Nothing communicates better than an earned cliché.

[Before we move on to the out chorus, listen to **2-3: E-I**, and then to the whole chart up to this point, **2-4: A-I**. Does it feel like we are building up to something inevitable? Our first chorus was the exposition, the solo chorus did some developing, and now we are about to put everything together before we recap.]

The Shout Chorus

Letters **I** through **J** have Denzal singing the first half of the song, but in a very different relationship to the band than in the first chorus. Where he sang the pick-ups in the first chorus with the horns answering, this time around, he and the horns reverse roles—the horns have the calls, and Denzal has the responses for the first 4 bars. In order to keep it simple and swinging, I used *tutti* voicings in **H8-I3** and then again in **I7-J1**. Where necessary, I used chromatic passing chords to keep things sounding interesting. The unison saxes bring back the 5th motif in **I5-6** and shrink it slightly to a flat 5th.

J starts with an anticipated Charleston. **J2** is identical to **B2**. The explosive brass hit with the fall-off in **J3** is to add excitement. We are building to the climax. The saxes in **J3-4** take over the role the bones had in **B2-3**. It's nice how it comes a measure later this time. Again this messes with the symmetry. **J5-6** has the bones returning to their 9th chord pecks (always the same voicing), but this time they have been reduced to one peck per bar. Each peck answers the vocal. **J7** has the same brass as **B7**. The saxes omit the pad from **B7** and join the brass on the last two notes, but with a higher voicing than before.

The Recapitulation

The dramatic break in **J8** leaves Denzal in the clear for his pick-ups to the recap. The *DS* covers the first 12 bars of the second half of the song, whereupon we go to the coda for the tag ending.

The Coda

The tag ending takes bars **29-30** of the song, sequences them up a half step but using *ii V*'s instead of chromatically descending dominants, and then repeats **D5-6**. The bones use half plungers this time, to evoke more of a feeling of comfort—sort of like coming home at the end of a long day, taking off your shoes and putting on your plush slippers. The upward diatonic scale in the trumpets and saxes harks back to **B7**, **C7** and **J7**.

This time however, it doesn't end short, but moves immediately to an E♭13 chord in the trumpets. This is startling because we are expecting a short *and* of 4 in the previous measure, and also, because the trumpets are suddenly left by themselves, harmonized in their upper register, which creates a spectacular high-wire act with no net below. They are then joined by everyone for a unison *"sol, do"* on the 4th beat, which is the highest note in the piece for the 1st Trumpet.

The Final Motivic Statement

The use of the motif in the last 3 bars of the chart was the only conscious decision I remember making in this chart. Everything else was pretty much instinctual. I wanted this last statement of the motif to feel like a slower tempo, thus giving a feeling of finality. Rather than change tempos, I augmented the note values, so it feels slower, but the beat actually remains the same.

The pitches in the 1st Alto are the opening 4-note motif of the song transposed up a step and then down to the 6th (our happy note). The chromatically descending dominants (F9+11, E7+5+9-9, E♭7-5-9) lead to a surprise D° (tonic diminished), which resolves to the final D69. For a little extra treat, I used upper structure triads on the E♭7 and D° (A/E♭7 and D♭/D with an E in the melody). The bass makes the final cut-off.

[Time for a final listen to **2-1: Complete Arrangement**. See if it feels satisfying. I ask myself, "Does this chart and performance get across the story in the lyric?"

I'm not sure this is what Irving Berlin and Florenz Ziegfeld had in mind. I don't think the idealized pretty girls they had on display 100 years ago were presented in such a swinging fashion, but that is my taste in music and women. I wasn't trying to write a period piece. Nor was I trying to describe the porn fantasies all too common in today's popular music. Call it what you will, but this chart is what Ellington used to describe as "a real swingin' chick." She's pretty, sexy, stylish, smart, hip, has a wry sense of humor and above all, is great fun to hang with.]

All At Sea

The author working on an arrangement. Photo ©2012 by Dion Tucker, courtesy of DavidBergerJazz.com.

3. All At Sea

[At www.suchsweetthundermusic.com/pages/cjca2-accompanying-files listen to **3-1: Complete Arrangement.**].

When I composed this song, I started with the idea that the title would be *I've Got My Eye On You.* I conceived of it as a Walter Donaldson sort of thing; very 1920s *(My Baby Just Cares For Me, My Blue Heaven)* but dressed up in a 1950s arrangement. When I gave it to Paul, he tried to write lyrics to my title, but came up empty. As usual, he suggested a better title, and wrote lyrics to it in no time flat. The undulating chromatics do sound much more nautical than anatomical. Sometimes your collaborators can know or feel certain aspects of a song better than you do yourself. If you keep an open mind, you may be surprised. It's only natural to resist someone messing with your creation, and the suggested changes are not always helpful, but I can think of a number of instances where collaborators helped me to see the potential in my own music.

Such was the case when I worked on *Harlem Nutcracker* with the brilliant choreographer Donald Byrd. Donald made very few changes to the score, but he had the vision of where to place the individual pieces, and how to insert different material within other material. He extended one eerie chart into a full-fledged brawl, and choreographed that entire fight scene without music. We videotaped the scene, and I then composed the music to *Attack Of The Ghouls* to fit the form and content of his wild choreography. That was the last number to be written for the show (just a couple of days before the first orchestra rehearsal and opening night). It remains one of my favorite numbers in the show.

All At Sea is a straightforward 32-bar *aaba* song form with very standard chord changes that can be found in a slew of songs. What makes it fun for me is the development of the 3-note chromatic motif: *la, le, sol* (which coincidentally is the inversion of the motif of *Stompin' On A Riff*, which is dealt with in Volume 1 of this series). It's very gratifying to me to write songs that use so little material. It's a challenge to keep finding interesting places to take the motif and keep it feeling surprising and fresh (*Example 3-1*, next page).

It just occurred to me that many of my tunes are based on motifs made up of minor 3rds and minor 2nds, which leads me to ponder... why these two intervals? I think the answer is my love of the blues. The ascending blues scale is made up of a minor 3rd, major 2nd, two minor 2nds and a minor 3rd. Although there is a major 2nd, it is the minor 3rds and minor 2nds that give the blues its distinctive character.

The Intro

I don't waste any time. The intro starts off with the motif, only backwards (retrograde). Instead of C, C♭, B♭, we have B♭ B, C in the first measure. You could also say that this is the inversion of the motif. The rhythm is identical to the motif at letter **A**: 8th rest, dotted quarter and two quarter notes, except that instead of repeating the motif and sequencing it, I just land on a tonic downbeat. The two most

33

LEAD SHEET

ALL AT SEA

Berger and Mendenhall

Example 3-1: Lead sheet

important and defining notes of this phrase are the first and last (B♭, which is the dominant of our key of E♭, and E♭, the tonic). The opening phrase is repeated with a different harmonization.

Rhythmic Displacement

The saxes then take over from the *tutti*, but where the *tutti* was harmonized in 4-part close moving around the cycle of 5ths or down chromatically, the saxes play 5-part open voicings in parallel motion before cadencing on the ♭*II7* (E7+9). After using rootless voicings for the tutti, the saxes sound so much richer on their answer, with the bari on the roots at the bottom. Also, note that the saxes play the 3-note motif three times. The rhythm is displaced, so that each time it has a slightly different rhythm and starts in a different place in the bar. The last three notes they play start on the same B♭, but then arpeggiate the tonic triad over harmonies that make the melody sound interesting.

Call-and-response

Another big element of the intro is the call-and-response with the drums: 1+1, 1+1, 3+1. I'm very concerned with construction. I mostly deal with 8-bar phrases. In order to make the music sound less predictable, I often use different size building blocks and overlap to obscure the foursquare nature of most jazz and standard songs. Sometimes it might be a simple construction like 2+2+4 or 1+1+2, but it could also be 2+3+1+2 or 3+3+2. Whatever the construction, it should always feel natural and not contrived.

Reading the Tea Leaves

When I wrote the intro, years ago, it felt right, but it wasn't until now, when analyzing it, that I realized that the whole chart is foreshadowed in the intro: the chromatic motif, the repetition and the prominence of the dominant and tonic pitches. All I knew back then was that I wanted to use the 3-note chromatic motif in some way. My subconscious supplied the rest. Over the course of my life, my subconscious was fed large doses of everything from Bach to Stravinsky, Gershwin to Ellington.

The Melody Chorus

Let's take a look at the melody of **All At Sea**. The first three notes are the main motif: C, C♭, B♭ (two descending minor 2nds). The entire song is derived from these three notes. In **A2** the motif is repeated in a slightly different rhythm before it returns to the first note. **A3** brings our motif down a 4th before returning to C once more. This time C is down the octave. The lower neighbor, B♮, and return to C are the first and second notes of the motif (C, B) and a return to C. **A4** is a repeat of the motif down a 4th from the previous measure.

A5 stays with the G, repeats the B♮, C from **A3** (hinting at both the retrograde and inversion of our motif) and returns to the G. **A6** is the full retrograde. **A7** returns to the F from **A4**, touches the tonic (E♭) before cadencing on the 6th (the C starting note of the song We wind up where we started, except down an octave.

The first six bars of **B** are identical to **A**. **B7** centers around the chromatics of our motif but transposed down a major 6th and with two added pitches—the initial D and then B♭.

The bridge at **C** uses the same rhythm as the first 2 bars of **A**. However, the motif is inverted and a 5th lower. This 2-bar figure repeats. **C5** is like **C1** except that the intervals are slightly expanded from minor 2nds to major 2nds. C6 repeats using the rhythm of **A2** and C2 before turning around in the opposite direction. The break on the downbeat of **C7** returns to our old friend G from **A3-5**. The rest of **C7** extends the idea of **A5**, inserting a tonic (E♭) before the inversion/retrograde of the motif a whole step higher (and metrically displaced) than **C1**. Naturally it ends on G—familiar territory.

Letter **D** is identical to the first six bars of **A** and then cadences on the inversion/retrograde transposed so that it ends up on the tonic (E♭).

Using Repetition to Your Advantage

As I've said before, I generally opt to repeat as much as possible. If repeating sounds good and feels satisfying, I'll go with that. However, when repetition sounds predictable, I've got to change things up, and maybe not that much—just enough to be surprising. This song is a great example. The listener can't help but understand the form and remember the tune because of how often the motif comes back. Honestly, writing this melody didn't take more than 10 or 15 minutes. The first measure came immediately, and the rest was simple. I just sang it, and wrote down what I sang.

The Opposites

I wasn't thinking about it while I was writing this chart, but now when I look at how the music develops, it's obvious to me that chromatics and repetition (of pitches, rhythms and both together) are the central ideas that are developed—the gradual change of pitch in the chromatic motif and the constancy of repeated pitches and rhythms. Listen to how these opposite ideas are pitted against each other, combined and ultimately made one by the time we arrive at the end of the piece.

Adding Harmony

After writing the melody, I started at the top and added the roots of the chords. Again, I wanted to keep it simple and in the tradition of the happy-go-lucky songs of the 1920s. The basic chord progression is very standard. There are hundreds of tunes with these chord changes. The general outline didn't take more than a few minutes. I spent maybe a half hour playing the tune over and over, deciding if and when to add passing chords that would dress up the harmony a bit.

For instance, the normal thing to do in **A5-8** is | E♭ Cm7 | Fm7 B♭7 | E♭ Cm7 | Fm7 B♭7 |. The roots don't work well with the melody (the C's in the melody collide with C's in the bass and the E♭ on beat 2 of the 7th bar is in unison with the bass), so I made some adjustments: F9 instead of Cm7 in **A5**, and then used some dominant 7ths to get to the Gm7 (deceptive cadence). Using a G♭7-5 substitute for Cm7 avoids the melody/bass unison and suggests some nice chromatic harmony. I thought about using a G♭° in that spot instead; it would have worked nicely, but I liked the sound of G♭7-5 better. The chromatic tritone resolution and the ♭5 seemed more in character for this song. Then the E7 tritone sub sounded less obvious, and again, more in character, than the dominant (B♭7).

Letter **B** is quite similar to **A**, except that it cadences on the tonic instead of using a deceptive cadence. The tonic is approached chromatically from below, using dominant 7th chords. This is followed by a *ii V* into the *IV* chord at the start of the bridge (|| Eb Bbm7 | Eb7+5 || Ab). Normally the *ii* chord in a *ii V* progression is sounded on a stronger beat than the *V* (such as: | E♭ | B♭m7 E♭7+5 || A♭). I have reversed it here in order to go with the surprise D♭ in the melody. The result is a big syncopation (2 beats + 6 beats).

The bridge is straightforward. |IV|ivm|I|V|vi |vi|vi|V/V| and then the basic changes in the last bar of the bridge are B7 B♭7. I used the standard thumb line on the Cm (C, B, B♭) but then, instead of moving down to the A, I repeated the V/vi vi progression that leads to the V/V (F9). For this chorus I used a chromatically descending chord progression to lead back to the tonic at D, rather than the more obvious harmonies that the melody suggests (A7 A♭7 G7 G♭7 F7 E7 E♭ rather than B7 B♭13 E♭). We can use those basic changes on the next chorus.

The New Orleans Break

How many New Orleans tunes from 100 years ago have a 2-bar break at the end of the *b* section? *Tiger Rag* comes to mind immediately. This convention found its way into Tin Pan Alley with such songs as *I Can't Give You Anything But Love* and *Honeysuckle Rose*. I like breaking on the *V/V*. It challenges us to hurry up and get back to the tonic in time.

Delaying the Final Cadence

Letter **D** (the last *a* section of the song) is like letter **A**, except that I have delayed the final cadence. The tonic doesn't occur until the downbeat of the 8th bar. This was done to go with the upwardly chromatic melody approaching the tonic. Rather than have the bass move parallel to the melody, I used contrary motion—chromatically descending dominants and then continue around the cycle of 5ths, before *ii V*-ing into the next chorus.

[I suggest you play the melody and chord roots for this melody chorus. Do you see how complete it feels with just the melody and bass? Now add 3rds and 7ths to your chords. These notes add color without disturbing the structure.]

Getting Started

My next step was writing out a lead sheet (melody and chord changes). I recorded myself playing it on the piano and emailed the mp3 to Paul. (We had made the title change by this time.) Later that night, he emailed a set of lyrics that fit perfectly. Sometimes minor ad-

Denzal Sinclaire rehearsing. Photo ©2009 by Nina Schwartz.

justments need to be made to the melody, lyric or both, but that was not the case here. I added the lyrics to my lead sheet and emailed it to Denzal. He wrote back that E♭ was his best key for this song.

At this point I could start scoring. I wrote out the melody, words and chord changes for the melody chorus (letters **A** through **D**) on my score paper. I write in pencil and keep an eraser handy, in case I change my mind. The melody and words are solid, but I might want to make some alterations or additions to the chord progression. All this will be the result of the backgrounds I create for the horns.

Achieving Balance

The sheer simplicity of the melody and harmony encourages me to be creative with the orchestration. Complicated songs don't need much in the way of accompaniment. Conversely, plain or simple songs can be made special with creative orchestration. It's the law of opposites. We don't want to overwhelm listeners, nor do we want to bore them.

"The three most important things in jazz are Rhythm, Rhythm and Rhythm—in that order."
Chuck Israels

Counterpoint

Since our melody is already in place (Denzal will take some liberties, but I don't concern myself with that), I need to create parts for the other 15 musicians that will make him sound good and help him to tell the story. Just as my harmonies were constructed in relation to the melody, my next step is to create interesting rhythms and countermelodies that serve the melody without stepping on it or obscuring it. Let's look at the first 8 bars (letter **A**).

My overriding contrapuntal principal is opposition. If the melody rests or holds onto a note, the countermelody moves, and vice versa. I try to find the holes and fill them—well, not all of them. I don't want the background to be predictable or too busy. Notice how the rhythms in the horns fill in where the voice isn't active. Starting right on the downbeat of **A1**, the bones have a solid punch for Denzal to bounce off of. In **A2** the bones reverse that order and react to Denzal on the *and* of 1. The next notes are in rhythmic unison with voice. I try not to do this very much for two reasons:

1. The confluence takes away the independent nature of the vocal.
2. The horns can obscure the words.

In this case, the rhythmic unison is very short-lived so, no harm, no foul. The next three trombone notes are in opposition to the vocal rhythms. The brass punctuation at the end of **A4** sets up the next phrase, where I switch over to the saxes. Although the saxes and voice are together on beat 3, and on the *and* of beat 4, this is obscured by the vocal note in the middle (on 3 *and*) and by the scoop in the saxes. The horns rest in **A6** while Denzal sings the inverted motif in his low register.

Giving some space before it makes the turn-around in **A7-8** all the more effective. I can get fancy here, since Denzal isn't active. The bones have a bar to make their statement. They are answered by the unison saxes supported by a trombone chord when they re-enter on the *and* of 2.

Melodic Considerations for Backgrounds

Although my first instrument was the piano, I never developed a lot of chops. I was too distracted from practicing by playing the trumpet, and then, by arranging and composing. But, growing up, I remember musicians talking about the pianist "feeding the soloist." I learned to do this in order to be polite and make my friends sound good—to help them create good solos or vocal performances. When I started arranging, I assigned a lot of my comping function to the horns.

I figured out how to orchestrate the sort of stuff I was playing on the piano to fit the horns at hand, and how to give the horns material that was idiomatic to both their instruments and the style of the piece. 50 years later I'm still at it. I may be a little more skilled at making everything more integral, but essentially I'm playing the same game. Our lead trombonist, Wayne Goodman, has pointed out on several occasions that the bones can "do more than be a pianist's left hand." Although I often need that function from them, I try to write them fun melodic material as well. Everyone loves to play melodies.

Serialization

Serialization is how we order things. It can be applied to all the elements in music: rhythm, melody, harmony, and orchestration. On the most basic level, we play a constant game of expectation and surprise. We create enough sameness to lure the listener, then we change things to surprise him. This is a basic human response, and forms the basis of comedy. I'm not sure to what level other animals can do this, but I think most mammals are capable of expectation and surprise. In any event, we generally perform for humans, who are suckers for this game.

Pretty Good is not Good Enough

I know that the rhythms are in good shape when they are swinging. If they don't feel quite right, I will consider alternatives.

Chuck Israels says that Bill Evans once told him that when you have two good solutions, and you are having a difficult time deciding which one to choose, this means that there is a third and much better alternative that you haven't thought of.

The term "serial music" has been misinterpreted to mean exclusively atonal music. Although atonal music is generally serial in nature, the idea of creating tone rows does not need to be limited to 12-tone rows, nor does it necessarily preclude tonality.

Stravinsky, for one, used rows with half that many notes, or less, to great advantage. I have at times used formal serial technique with anywhere from 5 to 12-note rows. The great

majority of my writing is conceived in a less formal way. I start with a motif and let the melody unfold. Good melody writing involves sensitivity to direction and the return of pitches. It's not only which notes you choose, but when.

[Let's look at the first trombone part from **A1–A4**. This is a satisfying line in itself. It has nice direction and some drama when it goes to the non-diatonic B♮, which then resolves chromatically upward to the 6th of the tonic E♭ chord. Next, play this part along with the melody. They complement each other nicely. The trombone stays away from the vocal pitches and has many of the colorful notes of the harmonies that are missing in the vocal line. Now play this trombone part along with the roots of the chords in the bass. Again, the trombone stays off the roots. There are mostly 3rds mixed with some 5ths and 6ths. The lower neighbor D in **A3** is a nice touch in that it is the +11 of the A♭ chord.

Now play the second trombone part. Play it against the lead trombone, the bass, and then the vocal. Also pretty good, right? Inner parts are important. As I've said before, everyone likes to play a melody. Now play the third bone part. I've given him all roots, except for the two unison notes in **A3**. Play his part against each of the other parts.

Now play all three bones and the vocal line together. Everything makes sense both vertically and horizontally. Each has a pleasing melodic part that fits together nicely with the other trombones, with the bass, and with the vocal. I treated these four bars as 4-part harmony between the vocal line and the three bones. The bass walks the changes, the piano fills in the cracks and the drummer plays time.

I recommend checking your work like this and making the necessary adjustments to satisfy the horizontal and vertical requirements. Sometimes I check during the arranging process, and sometimes I check when the entire score is completed.]

Voicing the Trombones

The bone voicing on the downbeat of **A1** is a root position triad. Since the vocal is going to come in a half beat later with the 6th of the chord, I want to stay off the 6th, if possible. The next two voicings have the root in the third trombone and the 3rd and 7th in the other bones. Again this works fine against the vocal that has the 9th on the B♭m7 and the +9 on the A7. We then resolve to an A♭ triad in the bones while the vocal moves chromatically down from the major 7th to the 6th. The two chromatic unison notes are a melodic reference—a 2-note fragment of our 3-note motif, but in contrary motion and down a 5th.

I had thought about using an A♭m triad, since the vocal again moves chromatically down from the major 7th to the 6th, but I went with the 6th in the second bone because the voicing felt better to me, and made a more interesting and satisfying line for the second trombone. Using the A♭m triad felt too stagnant. The tritone between the B♮ and F in the A♭m6 creates more of a need for resolution. That voicing is repeated on beat 4 and then resolves with contrary motion in the second bone to an E♭6.

Adding the Trumpets

The trumpets join the bones for these last two voicings. I kept the trumpets in their middle register in close position above the bones. I'll save the fireworks (trumpet high register) for later. I want to start the melody chorus nice and easy, and then build. Putting the 2nd Trumpet on the root a major 2nd below the 1st Trumpet's 9th is unusual, but it makes for nice voice leading when they resolve up a step to the 6th and 5th of the E♭ chord. Notice how the bottom two trumpets are also in parallel major 2nds. I like interesting vertical structures. The resulting 7-part brass harmony adds temporary complexity.

Voicing the Saxes

The saxophone answer to the brass is the kind of thing that saxes do so well—scooping up to a 5-part voicing, holding it with vibrato, and then jumping down into a simple 4-part close doubled lead punctuation. The F13+11 voicing has the 3rd and 7th on the bottom (voiced straddling middle C) with a G major triad in the top three voices. The following Fm7 voicing has the root on top and is strictly 1, 3, 5, 7, 1). No tensions. Since the vocal is singing the 9th at that point, we have enough harmonic interest.

The Turnaround

In the old days it was the arranger's job to write intros, codas, modulations, and turnarounds on vocal charts. The singer was inactive during these moments, so it was the band's time to shine. The rest of the chart could be footballs (whole notes)—either unison thumb lines or voiced out in pads. Thousands of published stock charts used this formula for 40 years. Stock arrangements were not very interesting, but they were at least functional. I still respect the logic that governed them. I know when the band's moments are, and try to give them as much fun as I can.

This turnaround (**A7-8**) brings back the bones similarly to what they played in **A3**, and then has the saxes answer them in unison (this is the first time in the chart that we hear unison saxes) while the bones punch out a tritone sub voicing.

Let's start with the bones. Their unison chromatic pick-up in **A7** is reminiscent of **A3**, except that it happens a beat and a half earlier in the bar. The following G♭13 voiced in 4ths is their meat and potatoes. While the second and third bones hold out their tritone, the lead trombone moves down from the 13th to the 5th before joining the other two in an Fm11 voicing.

Note that the vocal is holding a C during all this (the +11 on the G♭7 and the 5th on the Fm11). The vocal C freed me from having to use the C in both voicings. The Fm11 voicing is a bit unusual, but sounds effective due to the voice leading. I'm not sure why the bones didn't scoop their notes on the *and* of 2. To me it seems like the natural thing to do. Maybe I should have notated it for them, but they sounded good without it, so I didn't say anything.

After these two dissonant voicings, it feels most satisfying to go to a plain E7 (root, 7th, 3rd) in the bones in **A8**. The interest is both in the low E in the 3rd Trombone (the lowest note on his instrument) and the unison sax line that, after the first note, hits all tensions (5, 7, 11 on the Fm7) if you consider that their B♭ on the *and* of 2 hits with the bone E7 (+11, 9, +9, +5, +9). I've introduced this contrapuntal complexity in the turnaround that can be continued in the next *a* section, where the vocal line is added on top.

The Fun Begins

Denzal sings, "I lose my bearings," which prompts me to reflect that sentiment in the saxes. I continue with the unison saxes versus harmonized bones all the way into **B5**, so that they overlap the phrases on both ends (**A8** precedes **B1** and **B4** extends over the bar-line into **B5**). The saxes represent the chaos while the bones offer stability. Let's look at the saxes first.

I'm looking for a swirling effect. In **B1** the unison saxes play two inverted motifs—starting on the tonic and then on the dominant. In the next measure they repeat the last note of **B1** before playing a 2-note truncated motif starting on the subdominant and a 3-note motif starting on *re*. Although this sequence of the motif ends up on *do* (E♭), the harmony has moved to the subdominant (A♭), so it is now the 5th of the chord.

B3 continues with two 2-note truncated motifs (B♮ to C and G to A♭) before arpeggiating up the A♭maj7 to the 9th of the A♭m. The chromatic turn on the first two beats of **B4** is an altered motif. The following downward A♭m6 arpeggio circles the B♭ on the downbeat of **B5** and also provides the upper neighbor to the final tonic on the *and* of 1. These upward and downward arpeggios give a welcome relief to the upward and downward stepwise motion.

The trombone chords fit hand and glove (rhythmically and harmonically) with the sax line, either giving them a rhythmic goose, as in **B1**, or catching their accented notes. In both cases I avoided using the sax pitches in the bone voicings, so that the unison saxes and the three bones create 4-part harmony between them. This is a basic contrapuntal principle. You'll find it throughout Ellington and Strayhorn's music. I especially like the A major triad in the bones with the saxes playing the 7th and Denzal singing the +9. Triads bring out the trombones' nobility. Each section (bones, saxes, vocal) has its own personality. This is true counterpoint. The bone sonorities sound complete. Notice how the A♭m6 resolves smoothly to the E♭69, which is voiced in 4ths.

Turning It Over to the Brass

After this active sax line, I feel a craving for a brass answer. First, the trumpets and bones unite for a 2-note punctuation in **B5**. In this spot 8 bars earlier, the saxes played the same dotted quarter/8th note rhythm, but with the melody descending. This time I've got seven brass (four trumpets plus three trombones). I'm going to go with upper structure triads in the trumpets to create a bright yet complex sound.

On the **F7** the trumpets play a G major triad over the basic F7 sound in the bones (1, 3, 7). Since I only need three notes in the trumpets, I double the 1st and 2nd Trumpet on the 9th of the chord. The lead moves up a 3rd to the 11th of the Fm7, while the 2nd Trumpet stays on a common tone G, which is now the 9th of Fm7. This enables the 3rd and 4th Trumpets to ascend stepwise to the 7th and 5th of the Fm7.

Both the 1st and 3rd Trombones stay on their pitches (7th and root of Fm7), while the 2nd Trombone slides down a half step from the major 3rd of F7 to the minor 3rd of Fm7. The combination of parallel, contrary and oblique motion is most effective for this dramatic punctuation. The bitonality is another asset—the trumpets say G to Cm7 (*V i* in Cm), while the bones have F7 to Fm7.

Breaking the "Rules"

I've said that it is rare to double the voice in the horns, but there are times that it can be so delicious. Hey, Puccini doubled the voice constantly, and it worked well for him.

The first six beats of **B6-7** have the 1st Trombone doubling the voice. I didn't actually set out to do this. I had the words and melody in place, and then wrote the bass line. The 2nd and 3rd Trombones have natural harmony parts. I didn't want any more notes in the harmonies. They felt satisfying with the 4-part harmony between the vocal, bass and two bones. I added the lead trombone in unison with the voice to strengthen the harmonic effect of these chords. The bones must keep their volume down so as not to cover Denzal's vocal, which is in his low register. I wouldn't use unison with the voice for a longer passage, but for four notes, it seems just right.

"The Ellington Effect"

The harmony of these six beats is an example of what Billy Strayhorn used to call "The Ellington Effect." The B♭ melody is the -5 of the E7, which is the tritone substitute for B♭7 (V in our home key of E♭). Rather than staying on that chord until the resolution to the E♭ tonic on the downbeat of the next measure, I approached the E♭ chord chromatically from below (D♭7, D7, E♭). The complex E7-5 mov-

Duke Ellington in New York, 1946. Photo by William Gottlieb. Source: Library of Congress.

ing to a pair of plain 7th chords (no added tension) and then resolving to the surprise major 7th of the tonic in the melody has that beautiful melding of the simple and complex, done in such a way that the simple 7th chords sound special.

Covering up the Seam with Suspense

In order to move smoothly into the bridge and distract us from the 8+8+8+8 structure of this song, I created an instrumental answer (or, being Jewish, an instrumental question) in answer to the question, "What good's a compass..." The brass sting on the *and* of 3 in **B7** and then relax into their whole note in **B8**, while the saxes play three chromatic unison pick-ups, easing us up to the 3rd of the subdominant (C on the A♭ chord). I wanted the brass to move as little as possible in their *ii V* to A♭. The lead trumpet and bones have common tones, while the other three trumpets slide down a half step.

The B♭m7 voicing has the brass voiced in 3rds (1, 3, 5, 7, 9, 11) with the 11th doubled at the bottom. The result of the oblique motion into the E♭7 chord is that major 7th and minor 9th intervals are created between the B♮ and E♮ in the 2nd and 4th Trumpet and the E♭'s and B♭ in the players that hold onto their common tones. The tension built into this chord begs for resolution. To add to the suspense, the saxes play alterations of the 5th (-5, natural 5, +5) ascending chromatically up to the 3rd of the A♭ chord. The 3rd is the "sweet" note of any major chord, so it is especially welcome after all this tension.

The Thumb Line: Our Security Blanket

The unison saxes play a chromatic thumb line from **B8** through **C7**. Although this is the bridge of the song, this thumb line is made up

of our 3-note motif in augmentation: C, C♭, and B♭. These motivic pitches are framed on both sides by A♮'s (one more half step).

How is that for organic development? Once again, until this moment, I hadn't even realized that the thumb line contained our motif! I was just creating a colorful line that sounded good against the melody and bass. There is a sense of calm and security due to the long notes and chromatic movement. The serenity of this section is in direct contrast to the *a* sections, which describe more turbulent seas.

Vocal/Brass Call-and-Response

The 2-bar vocal phrases are all given 2-note long/short answers by the brass, varying the rhythm each time. The third answer is directly followed by a brass downbeat to punctuate the break in the rhythm section. The 1st Trumpet avoids the melody notes in the vocal as well as the thumb line in the saxes in order to establish independence. The only root in the 1st Trumpet is his first note, and that quickly resolves to the 3rd of the next chord.

Voicing the Brass

Let's now look at the brass voicings. I always consider the brass as both one entity and two sections (trumpets and trombones) acting together. Each section has its own sonority.

When I was in the Ellington band, we played *Satin Doll* every night. The brass chord in measure **8** fascinated me. It's an A7-9. The trumpets have (top down) A, E, C# and B♭, while all three bones play a unison A just below the bottom trumpet.

This was a revelation to me. I had always thought that seven players should play seven pitches, and have no unisons except, maybe, at the octave. One performance aspect of this combination of harmonized/unison voicings is that the harmonized voices will play their parts with personality and vibrato, while the unison voices will be impersonal, without vibrato (or what Duke would call "dead tone"). The combination and integration of disparate ideas is not only an advanced concept, but also one of the signs of the Maestro's greatness.

With this concept in mind, **C2** is voiced with the trumpets playing a simple A♭m6 in 4-part close position with the three bones on a unison B♭. B♭ is both the 9th of the chord (creating a minor 9th interval with the C♭ (B♮) above it in the 4th Trumpet) and the dominant of the upcoming E♭ chord. The trumpets resolve smoothly to a simple E♭6 in close position, while the bones play the same 4ths voicing they had on the downbeat of **B5**.

The G7 in **C4** has the top three trumpets in an upper structure E♭ major triad. Actually, the brass is voiced in 3rds starting on the 7th in the 2nd Trombone (7, -9, 3, +5, 1, +9). The 3rd Trombone is on the root. The following Cm7 chord also has the top three trumpets in an upper structure triad. This time it's a B♭ major triad. Again, if we overlook the 1st Trombone for a moment, everyone is voiced in 3rds (1, 3, 5, 7, 9, 11). I gave the 1st Trombone the 11th to strengthen the 1st Trumpet (by doubling him at the octave), to create a satisfying sonority in the bones, and to create a good shape to his line. It's important to me that each player has a satisfying line that sounds good against the bass and all the other brass parts.

The **C4-5** brass voicings are repeated in **C6** before resolving to the F13 in bar **C7**. Instead of giving the trumpets an upper structure triad, I open up the spacing and double the lead an octave lower in the 3rd Trumpet. This makes a strong punctuation.

By the way, I am not concerned with how the sax unison notes fit into the brass harmonies. We hear them as separate entities, just as we hear the vocal and bass as separate from the brass voicings.

Dressing Up the Break

Since the harmonies have to get to a B♭7 in **C8**, I go a step further and give the saxes and bass a chromatic pick-up in contrary motion to the vocal. The 1st Alto has the 3-note motif starting on E♭ and then two 2-note motifs (E♭ to D and G♭ to F). The other saxes are full of chromatics as well. The voicings start in 4-part close over roots in the bari and then open up into the cadence.

Brass vs. Saxes

Letter **D** pits the brass vs. the saxes in a variety of 2-note rhythmic figures. First the saxes play a tonic 69 chord in 5-part spread harmony. The bones answer in close harmony. Since Denzal is singing the +9 on the A7 and then the major 7th on the A♭ chord, I omit those pitches from the bone voicings. Note the contrary motion in the bones. I like how the 7th of the A7 resolves up to the 9th of the A♭ chord. The only movement in the bones on the chord on the *and* of 1 in **D4** is the 2nd Trombone moving chromatically down from the major 3rd to the minor 3rd. This is especially pungent because of the half step with the 9th in the 3rd Trombone.

The two full brass section chords that follow divide the brass in an interesting way. The top three trumpets are in an upper structure triad (E♭/A♭m) and resolve to an incomplete E♭ structure (1, 2, 5—no 3rd). The bones and 4th Trumpet form more complete chords (A♭m6 with no 5th, resolving to E♭6 in Drop 2). The contrary motion between the ascending 4th

Trumpet and the descending bones adds some welcome complexity. The tonic and dominant pedal point in the 3rd and 1st Trumpets establishes a firm tonality.

Sax Copy Back

In **D5** the saxes repeat their chord from **A5**. If I find something distinctive, I like bringing it back if possible. This gives the piece character. In this case, I omit the sax downbeat from **A6**. That would feel too repetitious.

Trumpet Pedals vs. Bone Motifs

In **D6-7** the trumpets fan their derbies on repeated dominant pedals, sticking with the dominant pedals that the lead trumpet had in **D4-5**. These repeated dominant pedals create a fanfare-like effect as if to proclaim, "Here comes something good." Notice how the trumpets are repeating their pitch while at the same time the bones are playing the chromatic motif—concurrent opposites.

More Descending Chromatics for the Bones

While Denzal sings an upward chromatic line in **D6-7**, the bones descend chromatically in typical 13th voicings. This is standard fare for the trombone section—7, 3, 13. The weird thing here is the first trombone descending into the D (13th) on the downbeat of measure **D7** while the vocal ascends into C# (the augmented fifth). The contrary motion between them makes it work. After that the bones fill out 4-part close harmony below the vocal, resolving into the full cadence.

[I suggest that you listen to **3-2: A-E** and review the material I have discussed at the same time. Does it feel like we have come to the end of Chapter One, and we want to find out what happens next? I hope so. I didn't want it to feel like the story had come to an end (although the lyrics do), so I threw in the repeated inverted dominant pedals in the trumpets in **D6-7**. Sneaky, right? Well, that's my job—to keep the listener in the game.]

Band Interlude

4-part Close/Doubled Lead Sax Soli

The saxes have been resting for a couple of bars while the brass assist the singer finishing his melody chorus. So now it's time for the saxes to take over. I wrote *"Soli"* on their parts so that they would know that they are playing the most important thing going on at that time, and so that they would stand up when they play this passage in concert. That way the audience would know to direct their eyes and ears toward the saxes and away from the singer.

The saxes take a 7-note pick-up into the second chorus. The entire 17-bar *soli* is voiced 4-part close, with the bari doubling the 1st Alto at the octave. This is classic sax soli scoring: think Ellington's *Cotton Tail*, Brookmeyer's *You Took Advantage Of Me*, Al Cohn's *Lady Chatterley's Mother* and *Air Mail Special*, and just about every sax soli until Thad Jones.

Thad hated two things: the clarinet, and 4-part close harmony. His solis are basically Drop 2. He had 5 saxes; the bari generally plays the Drop 2 part. The 4th Tenor doubles the 1st Alto at the octave (about 1/3 of the time), or plays a 5th harmony note. But we'll look at 5-part *soli* writing later. For now, let's focus on how to write 4-part close that doesn't sound dated—no easy feat.

Melody/Bass Relationship

I started off knowing the basic changes of the song, and wrote the lead line in the 1st Alto part. It's pretty much like an improvised solo, but the bar for motivic development is much higher for composing and arranging than it is for improvising. We'll see how well I did in a minute. I wrote 16 measures, after which I felt it was time to change texture and orchestration. I reserve the right to use passing chords (which happen a lot in this soli) and substitute changes (which don't happen here at all) to make the melody sound fresh and avoid weak melody/bass relationships and awkward inner parts.

Repeating Pitches

When I was young, teachers and books on arranging always said to avoid repeating pitches in the inside parts when the melody notes are moving. For the most part, I agree. Repetition on the inside can create awkward lines and inner melodies less interesting than the primary melody, as well as stagnant harmonies. So I avoided it for many years. After a while, I became fascinated with repeated notes in the melody coupled with moving parts and harmonies underneath. This led me to explore the possibilities of the reverse: moving melodies coupled with one or two repetitive inside parts. I found situations in Ellington's music where this happened, and I loved the sound of it.

When I wrote the first four notes at letter **F** (repeated E♭'s), I knew that I would use the classic stride piano harmonization *ii #ii⁰ I* for the first three notes. With that going on in my head, when I went to harmonize the beginning of the soli (pick-ups to **E**), I was hearing the same harmonies, only in a different inversion. Now the repeated E♭'s are in the second

voice instead of the lead. This inspired me to find more situations for repeated inner parts.

Of course I will make sure that the harmonies don't sound stagnant, and that each voice sounds melodic and relates well to the bass and the other saxes. The chromatics in the 1st Alto consist of two inverted motifs (the first starting on F, and the second in the original key—starting on B♭). When I use the repeated note idea, two saxes play the repeated notes, two play our inverted chromatic motif, and the bari doubles the 1st Alto down the octave. This occurs in **D8**, **E1**, **E4**, **F1**, **F3**, and **F6**. Using the same technique six times gives this soli character and unity.

Line Writing

Herb Pomeroy used to teach an advanced arranging course at Berklee called "Line Writing." The basic principle was to voice anchor chords and then connect them by creating a good melody for each player, without regard to what harmonies resulted from the confluence of these moving lines. The idea is that the strength of the anchor chords and the direction of the lines will make everything work.

I sometimes combine this technique with chords and voicings that I am familiar with. Sometimes it leads to unusual progressions. Such is the case in beats 3 and 4 of this pick-up. The resulting harmonies are Fm11 D♭7 B♭9+5 E♭6. The Fm11 voicing may look odd at first, because it contains both the minor 3rd and 11th and omits the root. If I used a root or 9th rather than the minor 3rd, it would sound like an F7sus4 rather than an Fm7, which is not what I want.

For the B♭7 chord on beat 4, there is a 9th in the melody. I employ an augmented fifth to give this chord more chromatic pull toward the Eb tonic resolution; the F# on the Bb7 will resolve up a half step to the G (the 3rd of Eb6). Never mind that the whole voicing jumps down. We sense this resolution of the F#. So my two anchor chords are Fm11 and Bb9+5. I now connect the individual notes using either repetition or stepwise motion, and voilà! The resulting chord is a Db7. Interesting. I wouldn't have thought of that chord.

[I suggest that you play the 7-note pick-up with each sax part by itself, with the bass notes (Eb, F, Bb) and then each part against each of the other parts, combinations of three parts, four parts and all five parts. Do you see how the individual lines converge to create chords, rather than starting with predetermined chords and trying to make the lines work melodically?]

Consistency

The next 16 bars follow suit—4-part close/ doubled lead sax voicings with as many repeated notes as makes sense. I've analyzed the individual voicings. Sometimes I thought of the harmony first, sometimes the line, but I always made sure that both sounded good— the horizontal lines and the vertical structures (voicings). I'm having fun being creative within the confines of creating a consistent overall sound for 16 measures.

There are lots of examples of the four types of approach chords: diminished, chromatic, diatonic, and dominant. Notice that I don't burden the rhythm section with the passing chords. Even if they could play them, it would interrupt the groove. The only passing chord I let the rhythm section in on is the Gb7-5 on beat 4 of **F5**. Also, note the liberal use of tensions and altered tensions. Finally, there is the deviation in texture in the last measure

of the *soli* where the 1st Alto plays a soloistic ornament. In a subtle way this sets up his improvised solo that starts four bars later.

The Send-off: Alternating Tonic Unisons with Mostly Dominant *Tuttis*

The Eb pickup to letter **G** is a band unison. Each instrument is placed in a comfortable register that will match the intensity of the trumpets. I omitted the 1st Alto, so that he can prepare to play his solo. The next three bars alternate tonic unisons with *tutti* voicings. The Bb's on the downbeats of each bar are the dominant of the key of Eb, but perform a different function in each chord (9th of Abmaj9, 9th of Abm6, and 5th of Eb6). This is a continuation of our technique of oblique motion (one or more voices repeat while the others move stepwise.

We then return to a tonic unison on beat 2 of **G3** before using a dominant approach (Bb7+9) to the final Bb (5th of Eb6). The +9 on the Bb7 is especially effective because it is a blue note (b7 in the key of Eb). This note sets up a bluesy tone for the alto solo. Notice how Jay Brandford picks this up in his solo in **G4-8**. We've had so much busy writing that I feel it's time for some space. The alto solos with accompaniment from just the rhythm section for these five bars.

Background Figures

The background riffs for the alto solo (**H1-4**) continue the technique of band unison tonics with a harmonized dominant (Bb). At **G** I did this on the changes of the bridge. Here at **H** it is over the *a* section. This is very unifying. The final chord in **H4** is not voiced *tutti*, as the previous voicings were. The top three trumpets are in 4ths over the 4th Trumpet and the trombones, who are also voiced in 4ths. The saxes are under the brass; the top two in 4ths and the bottom two in 5ths (inverted 4ths). I opted for a spread-out 69 voicing to put a period on the ensemble and signal that the solo is coming to a close. I let Jay and the rhythm section finish up by themselves for four bars before returning to the vocal accompanied by ensemble voicings.

[Let's listen to everything up to this point, **3-3: A-I**. Do you feel like we've had a nice trip and it's time to return home? Has the trip been satisfying and eventful? It wasn't meant to be especially exhausting or soul-searching; after all it's just a simple love song. I gave it a little bit of depth, but this song is about the start of a relationship, not the darker and more complex middle.]

The Recap

Rather than have Denzal sing a full chorus of melody for the recapitulation, I skipped the first 16 bars of the song and went directly to the bridge. This is fairly common—so much so that the universal signal for this is to touch the bridge of your nose with your forefinger.

Piano Signals

It was common practice in the Count Basie and Duke Ellington bands for the pianist/leader to play a signal to the band to let them know that the next section was coming up. These are short figures that are significantly different from what is going on at the moment. I have written such a signal for the piano in **H8**. It's our old friend the octave E♭'s. This time it appears in a pair of 8th notes in the piano, rather than a single E♭ octave unison in the horns, as we heard earlier in the first four bars of **G** and **H**. The same figure is repeated two bars later, but over different chords.

Riffs are most effective when the harmonies change beneath the repetitive melody, so that we hear each repetition of the melody in a different light.

Call-and-Response

The piano signals set up a call-and-response with the horns (omitting Jay, since he has just finished his solo). I've put the trumpets in their middle register, so as not to overpower the vocal. The piano 2-note call is answered by a 2-note response from the horns. I employ four basic opposites to distinguish the calls from the responses:

- Fast vs. slow—The piano is moving in 8th notes while the horns answer with dotted quarter/doubly dotted half note.
- Long/short articulation in the piano vs. long/long in the horns.
- Octave unison piano vs. harmonized horns (*tutti* voicings).
- Register—The horns answer the piano an octave and a half higher.

More Dominants (B♭'s) With the Same Voicings

Do you remember the *tutti* voicings at G under the B♭ melody notes: A♭maj9, A♭m69 and E♭6? Here is the same situation. We are on the bridge again. I've kept the same melody notes (repeated B♭'s) but lowered the brass an octave. Instead of voicing the saxes an octave below the trumpets (which is normal for high trumpet voicings), I couple the saxes starting with the 2nd Trumpet and voice down from there, so that the bari will double the 1st Trumpet at the octave (along with the 1st Trombone). This doesn't have as much weight as when the saxes are voiced lower.

Passing Off the Signal to the Horns

The horns finish their *tutti* passage by taking over the piano signal on beat 4 of **I4**. However, the lead trumpet plays repeated G's (the 3rd in the key of E♭, but even more importantly here, the 5th of Cm, the key of the moment). I used a flat fifth on the G7 leading to the tonic Cm6 to give it a little more interest and chromatic pull.

Motivic Chromatic Thumb Line

I5-7 has the saxes playing a chromatic thumb line ending in a harmonized button (**F7-5**). Their notes are a truncated 2-note motif followed by the full 3-note motif transposed a half step lower than the original. Here is a clear case of an earned cliché. The common alteration of a minor chord: Cm, Cm(maj7), Cm7, Cm6 ties in perfectly with our motif. So often this cliché thumb line is used gratuitously and feels cheap, but we welcome it here. The trombones answer with a 2-note chromatic motif in **I8**. The B9 and B♭9 chords are the original changes I had in mind for this spot, but I came up with something fancier in the first chorus, so here at last is the original that I promised you back then.

The Final *a* Section and Tag

Letter **J** is the final *a* section of the song. I'm going to start small, with just the voice and rhythm section for four bars, and then start building to a big finish. I have Denzal repeat, "You weave your spell" twice before finishing the phrase. The second time he sings this phrase, I re-harmonize it so that it feels like we are going somewhere, but we don't know where (after all, we are all at sea!).

There is an interesting melody/bass relationship here. Although I originally repeated the melody verbatim, Denzal took the liberty of changing it the second and third time. I like what he did, so I'm going to go with it. I especially like how in **J7** he sings the 7th of the A7 and then repeats that G so that now it is the major 7th, resolving down a step to the 6th of A♭ before going back up to G, which is now the +11 of the D♭7.

As long as I'm changing the vocal in **J7**, I'll change the 1st Trombone part. On the recording Wayne played a G (the major 7th of A♭) because Denzal was supposed to sing B♮ to C (C being the 3rd of the A♭ chord). But since Denzal is now on the major 7th, I'll move the 1st Trombone up to the C, so that they are not doubling the major 7th, and so that we get the richness of having a 3rd in the chord. As an added bonus, the 1st Trombone part is now Db, C, B♮, which is our motif transposed down a 3rd. It's nice when things happen naturally like that.

Changing Speeds

Now I'm going to start going crazy—or at least it will sound like I am—but actually it's a pile of chromatic motifs combined with changing speeds.

In **K1-2**, while the vocal and bones continue their usual harmonized dotted quarter followed by two quarter notes, the saxes go wild with unison descending 8th note versions of the motif. The bones finish on the downbeat of **K3** and the harmonized saxes take over, and change direction by playing upward chromatic 8th note motifs. The arpeggio on beats 3 and 4 of **K3** contains chromatic harmonies (B9, C13+11, B9, B9+11).

There is a repeated note near the start of this figure in the 2nd Alto, but after that it's all parallel textures until the last note. The middle three voices move in contrary motion into the dotted quarter in **K4**. While all this movement is going on in the saxes, the vocal stretches what were originally two half notes into two whole notes, and the harmony goes with him. This is classic augmentation to create more suspense going into the final cadence of a piece. Thank you, Mr. Beethoven!

Coda

While Denzal sings his final tonic, the trumpets and saxes play a *tutti* figure based on the inverted motif from the intro. I'm looking for power and brightness, so the trumpets are an octave higher than they were in the intro. The first two, beats of **K6** contain the same melodic pitches as **K5**, but in half as many beats and with a different syncopation. The unison bones hammer away at the dominant in the rhythmic cracks not being used by the trumpets and saxes. This serves to goose the trumpet/ sax figures. All the horns come together for the final 2-note cadence. Following the *tutti* voicings, these two complex voicings are most satisfying. The altered tones on the B♭7+5+9-9 create a lot of tension, and then resolve to a solid E♭69, which has the trumpets in simple

Count Basie at the Aquarium, New York, circa 1946-8. Photo by William Gottlieb. Source: Library of Congress.

4-part close with the bones tightly underneath them in 4ths. The bari is down low on the root with the other saxes voiced in 4ths, starting with the 4th Tenor on the 3rd (a 10th above the bari). The re-harmonization of **K5-6** adds to its wildness. Everything comes to a sudden halt with a break on the downbeat of **K7**.

The Basie Signature

Here is one of the most famous and overused clichés in all of jazz—the Basie signature. But once again, I've earned the cliché. The repeated tonics are on top of our inverted motif transposed to F—our central opposites being stated one last time. The bones shut the door with a surprise +9 chord. The 1st Trombone's F# is a continuation of the F, F#, G inverted motif. Now we are descending chromatically, hinting at the original motif, but stopping just before the last note of it—a real tease ending.

[Listen again to **3-1: Complete Arrangement**. I'm always surprised at how, when you analyze a piece and then listen to it again, if it is developed effectively, we don't really notice all that motivic development. It just feels satisfying.]

Sheet music cover, c. 1921. Source: Lester S. Levy Collection of Sheet Music, Johns Hopkins University Library.

4. All By Myself

[At www.suchsweetthundermusic.com/pages/cjca2-accompanying-files listen to **4-1: Complete Arrangement.**]

Here's another great Irving Berlin song. I set out to write this arrangement in the style of Sy Oliver. When I was growing up, my dad had a buddy who had been a drummer as a young man during the Swing Era. He and I would listen to Duke and Basie, but then he would say, "But my band was Jimmie Lunceford."

When I was a young man playing in bands, all the older cats would smile whenever Lunceford's name came up. I had never even seen a Lunceford record; all of his sides were long out of print. It would be another six years or so, around 1973, until MCA reissued the original Decca Lunceford sides. At that time I was on the road in Toronto. A few of the guys in the band and I went to a local record store and there they were—four Lunceford LPs that covered the hits from 1934-1942.

Jimmie Lunceford with trombonist Trummy Young, early 1940s. Photo by William Gottlieb. Source: Library of Congress.

As soon as I got back home, I listened to them over and over, learning every arrangement. I understood immediately what all the fuss was about. This was an arranger's band—mainly Sy Oliver and Eddie Wilcox. They had a huge influence on the writers who came up right behind them—Billy May, Marty Paich, Bill Finegan, Eddie Sauter and Gerald Wilson especially. Glenn Miller and Stan Kenton modeled their bands' styles on Sy's and Wilcox's charts. I later got to know Sy a little, but I never asked him who his influences were. From what I can hear, I'd say primarily Duke Ellington and Don Redman.

Although Sy wrote wonderful and very popular instrumentals like *For Dancers Only* and *Organ Grinder's Swing*, he had a special talent for vocals—for solo singers, trios, and quartets. His sly humor delights me to this day. *Opus One* and *On The Sunny Side Of The Street* (both written for Tommy Dorsey) were his biggest hits, and *Then I'll Be Happy* (also for Dorsey) is really sweet. But if I had to pick one chart of his, I'd have to say *Ain't She Sweet* from 1939, one of the last charts he wrote for Lunceford before departing for the much greener financial fields of Dorseyland.

Even by 1939, the 1927 song *Ain't She Sweet* was dated, but Sy recast it over the Lunceford rhythm section's infectious 2-beat feel and added clever rhythms and hip phrasing in the horns and vocals. The secret to the Lunceford band's vocal group sound is how softly they sang in either 3- or 4-part close harmony. None of them had developed voices, so they just applied the phrasing they used on their horns, got close to the mike, and kept their volume low.

When we first started playing swing dance gigs with our band in 1999, I wrote a chart on *Exactly Like You* with a vocal trio made up of three of the horn players in our band—an obvious homage to Sy Oliver. We recorded that chart on our **Doin' The Do** CD later that year. A few years later, when we recorded our CD with Champian Fulton, we added her to the vocal trio for *I Can't Give You Anything But Love*. And then, when a project came along to record public domain and original songs with Denzal and the band, this seemed like a perfect opportunity to do a follow-up.

I looked over my list of public domain songs (pre-1923) and **All By Myself**, with its limited range and short phrases, seemed a natural for the Lunceford style. I started by sketching the quartet chorus. Once that was done, I got out my score paper and started writing the intro. Like Sy's chart on *Ain't She Sweet*, I gave the alto sax a melody chorus and a 4-bar interlude, which sets up the quartet chorus. I deviated from Sy's chart after the quartet chorus; I needed to modulate down a major 2nd to the key of B♭ for Denzal. I also shifted gears at that point, and had the rhythm section go from 2-beat into 4. This final chorus, and especially the tag, reminds me of the records Bobby Darin made in the late 1950s and early '60s.

On the next page is the lead sheet I started with (**Example 4-1**). Let's take a look at what makes this song a standard. First there is a great lyric. "In a cosy Morris chair" was later changed to "with a table and a chair," but I prefer the original words. A Morris chair is basically an early recliner. Here's what Paul has to say about the lyrics:

"**All By Myself** is a good example of a Berlin demotic lyric—a lyric written in the language of the people. Lyrics before Berlin tended to be highfalutin, full of pseudo-poetry of the 'I am truly thine' type. This was particularly true of operettas, but even a popular song could have a title like *Drink To Me Only With Thine Eyes*— a proposition that seems to defy anatomy. (Alan Jay Lerner had a huge aversion to this kind of thing. The line, 'All at once my heart took flight' in *I Could Have Danced All Night*) embarrassed him until the day he died.

Berlin introduced a much more direct, unpretentious kind of song lyric, employing language that people actually used in their lives. **All By Myself** consists of a series of straightforward statements, leaving the emotional resonance to the music. It would be a pretty uninteresting lyric, in fact, were it not for the reference to a Morris chair, which gives it a specificity that saves it. All the more reason not to change it!

This preference for direct simplicity extends, in the case of this song, to the rhyme scheme as well, which is barely there. It breaks down like this: AB CDD EF GGF. It is a cliché that rhyme implies intelligence; it is also true that it implies a certain energy and positivity. This is a song for a simple, lonely, depressed person. So the loose structure and paucity of rhyme are entirely appropriate."

The Melody

It's amazing what Berlin can do with a melody that spans only an octave (*re* to *re*). There are 11 accidentals, so it's pretty chromatic: 3 D#'s, 3 F#'s, 3 A♭'s (G#'s) and 2 B♭'s (A#'s). The D#, F# and B♭ are all blue notes.

ALL BY MYSELF

Irving Berlin

Example 4-1: Conventional lead sheet.

The central motif consists of the first four notes, which say, "All by myself", the title of the song. The motif is sequenced a 3rd higher in the next bar, and jumps up a 4th rather than a 3rd. The first three bars of the song outline a first inversion tonic chord with chromatic lower neighbors to the 3rd and 5th.

Bar **5** resolves the tonic C down to B (the 3rd of G7, the dominant) before leaping down a 6th to D, E, F, repeating the title phrase. The D, E, F becomes the counter-motif. Rather than chromatic, it is diatonic. The basic pitches of these 4 bars are B, D, F, B and G: the four notes of a G7—the dominant of C. The final G functions as the 5th of the tonic chord, which is the original chord change in that measure. The E and A are diatonic passing tones.

So we see the first 4 bars of the song as the tonic with chromatic lower neighbors, and the second 4 bars as the dominant with diatonic passing tones. What an excellent setup of opposites to build a song on! The inversion of this counter-motif occurs in Bars **11**, **13**, **15**, **26**, **28** and **30**. Measures **6** and **22** use these pitches, but out of order (***Example 4-2***).

The entire rest of the song is a development of these pitches and rhythms.

I didn't envision using a verse, so I never even investigated what Berlin's verse is. I've never heard it on any of the recordings I know of this song. Very often, if I like a verse, I'll use it in a vocal arrangement. I even used the classic verse to Cole Porter's *Night And Day* in one of my instrumental arrangements of that song. When Champian and I recorded Berlin's *He Ain't Got Rhythm*, we started with the verse.

I sometimes write verses to my original songs—not my jazz tunes, but songs with words that are meant to be sung. Jon Hendricks and I wrote a verse to our *Never-The-Less* for Champian. Paul Mendenhall and I have written dozens of songs with verses. We even added lyrics and a verse to an unpublished Harry Warren song, *With Your Hand In Mine*. Although we had recorded an instrumental version of Warren's tune without a verse, when I started writing a vocal chart for Freda Payne, it cried out for a verse. I'll talk more about verses in a later chapter.

Getting Started

My process in starting an arrangement is generally to play the song on the piano until I can find an angle—a way of looking at the song that feels personal to me. This one came in bar **3**. Ever since I first heard *Take The A Train*, whenever I hear a *V* of *V*, I want to stick a +11 in it. I don't usually change the composer's pitches, but the D7 in bar 3 of **All By Myself** is crying out for a G#. So, since I'm the producer, I'm going to make the melody a +11 instead of a 7th. Besides, the G# is a half step above the previous G, which adds to the upward chromatic motion of the motif. Here's the vocal quartet as I sketched it to start (***Example 4-3***, next pages).

Voicing and Voice Leading Considerations

Bear in mind that, except for Champian singing the lead voice, the three guys singing the lower parts are not really singers. Ryan, Fletch and Matt bring their authentic jazz phrasing to the game, but I have to keep their parts easy to sing in vertical and horizontal terms. For voicings: I mostly stay away from half-steps or minor 9ths, and limit the use of major 7th intervals. All the lines must be very singable, with limited amounts of jumping around. Champian can do some leaps, but everyone else should repeat pitches, move stepwise or by 3rds for the most part.

Keeping common tones in instrumental writing is generally frowned upon, unless the melody also repeats. I like the texture of having two voices move by step while the other two repeat their notes. I also like having one

Example 4-2

ALL BY MYSELF vocal quartet

Example 4-3, Vocal quartet

© 2010 Such Sweet Thunder

voice repeat his note while the other three move.

The one tricky spot in this chorus occurs on the word "old-er." Champian jumps up a 5th, Ryan a major 2nd, Matt a tritone and Fletch a major 6th. The Ab7-5 voicing is very sophisticated, but Fletch has the only hard part. Moving to the Dm7, although they are all jumping up, is

not that hard to hear, because all the pitches in the Dm7 are diatonic.

Re-harmonization

I tried to limit my use of re-harmonization and pick my spots. I want this to sound tasty and not like a science project. I kept most of the basic chords in place. There is a bit of tritone

Vocal Quartet   2   All By Myself

substitution to avoid melody/bass unisons as well as *ii V* and minor *iim7-5 V* to dress up some of the dominants or to keep them from being stagnant.

Passing Chords

Diminished, chromatic, and dominant approaches are sprinkled throughout, to avoid repetitious, stagnant under-parts and to harmonize chromatic non-chord tones. The first three bars of letter **F** set the tone for the entire chart. It only took a few minutes to write the vocal parts for these measures, and the rest of the chart pretty much wrote itself.

Vocal trio, David Berger Jazz Orchestra, Detroit Jazz Festival 2014. Brian "Fletch" Pareschi, Matt Hong, Dion Tucker. Courtesy of DavidBergerJazz.com.

Texture

All the voicings in this chorus are either 4-part close or Drop 2 with the exception of that colorful A♭7-5 in **I5**, which is in Drop 3. The low A♭ root really has character. Jumping down with the syllable "old" is so natural.

Although the vocal parts primarily move in parallel or oblique motion, every now and then I sneak a bit of contrary motion into one of the parts just to spice things up and keep the singers and listeners on their toes. Let's look at measure **F6**. The standard second voice would be E♭ D C. By having Ryan move up to the E on the *and* of 3, rather than slide down in parallel motion to a D, I put a 13th in the G7 chord and then resolved that down to the 9th of the C chord instead of using the less interesting root. Also note that this C69 is now voiced in 4ths.

Passing the Lead Around

Although Champian sings the melody, after she is established, I gave each of the other three singers short melodic solos in **G6**, **G8**, **H8**, **I2**, **I4** and **I6-8**.

Solos add personality and change the listener's perspective. We identify with the soloist.

Instrumental Accompaniment

There is so much interesting stuff going on in this vocal quartet chorus, that I don't want accompaniment to compete with it or mask any of it. The drums play softly on the closed hi-hat while the bass is in 2 and the piano softly plays two-handed stride (oom-pahs). For just a little color, I have Dan Block play *chalumeau register* New Orleans clarinet filigree. This is both soft and transparent. (If I'd had an acoustic guitar, he could have either played four chords per bar, Freddie Green style, or softly soloed with tasty blues licks in place of the clarinet.) The solo clarinet is the one in this chorus who really *is* all by himself. Later on, in the next chorus, Denzal sings all by himself. It's of utmost importance to tell the story of the lyric.

Rhythmic Considerations and Word Painting

To further paint the picture of being alone, I've chosen to use short phrases with short last notes, thus leaving space. All of this word painting was subconscious at the time when I was writing this chart. I was aware of the lyrics, but didn't make any effort to reflect them in the music. It all just happened naturally. You don't want to overdo it (Mickey Mouse).

Back when I was ghostwriting for Al Cohn, he would sometimes hand me just a lead sheet. I once asked, "That's it? No instructions?" He said, "It's a vocal chart. It's not a band number. You could do a little word painting if you like. When the lyric says *trombones wailing,* give the bones something. I wouldn't worry about it too much." That was it. I was sorry I had asked. Al figured that things would happen naturally. Besides, I was never good at calculating. My humor is subtler than that. The goal is to be organic.

Now that I think about it, it's been very rare in my career that I was given instructions. All Ralph Burns said was that he liked horn backgrounds behind all the solos. When I worked for Quincy Jones, aside from the overall concept of the show, we would usually just discuss titles and instrumentation for each piece.

Working with directors and choreographers was more specific at times. They might say, "I need enough music for the dancer to get from here to there," or "I need you to catch these hits." They always left it to me to make it musical. I think it works out best that way. Although I can cook a bit, I would never go to a restaurant and tell a chef how to prepare my meal.

[Take a listen to **4-2: F-J** and see if we have captured that relaxed and sly Lunceford style. In terms of performance, the swing phrasing and understated approach are crucial. Notice the accents, and how soft the subsidiary notes are. This gives the music its coolness.]

Intro

Now that we know the character of this chart, let's go back to the top. The 8-bar intro utilizes riffs, call-and-response and a solo break. The plunger-muted brass riff is answered in the piano before the brass repeats their statement. This second time, they are answered by a 2-bar alto sax break. The passing diminished chords in the brass are the reverse of how they are used in the vocal trio. Instead of having the melody move chromatically, and two of the inner parts repeat their pitches, the top two trumpets repeat their pitches, while the next two voices move down and then up chromatically.

The 3rd Trombone and the bass repeat the dominant pedal. The saxes rest for the entire intro, so that the alto break feels very dramatic, since it is the first saxophone note we hear. Drastic changes in orchestration are immediately obvious to every listener, and so can be quite effective. I very often change orchestration at letter **A** of an arrangement to announce the melody. I want the listener to know when the intro ends and the melody begins.

Melody Chorus #1, Alto Sax Solo

Essentially this chart consists of: intro, alto sax melody chorus, 4-bar interlude, quartet melody chorus, solo vocal melody chorus with tag ending. In the first chorus, the alto plays the melody with answers from the plunger-muted brass alternating with sax pads every 8 bars. I'm only writing for 5 brass and 4 saxes here, because I need a trumpet, a bone, and a sax player to sing in the quartet on the next chorus. Rather than have them jump up and down, and move to and from the mic, I let them rest when they are not singing.

Developing the Intro Material

The basic scheme for the brass responses in this chorus is to stay with the concept of the intro: alternating closed/open plungers with as much repetition of pitches as possible. Melodic movement happens in the lower voices and is chromatic where possible. The lead trumpet never doubles the pitches in the alto melody, thus creating independence of parts.

The sax background at **B** utilizes harmonized pads for two bars, a 1-note answer in **B3**, a unison response (descending chromatics followed by a striking E♭ blue note and a final D9 voicing in **B5**.

The brass returns a bar early with a dramatic altered dominant voicing while the bass plays his fill. At **C** the brass reverses the call-and-response by going first. While they are at it, they take over the chromatics previously played by the alto—a simple chromatic approach—alternating C69 and B69. The D13+11 is preceded by its dominant, A7-9. The brass peck in **C5** is reminiscent of the same figure in the saxes in **B3**. The brass then returns to its repeated note answer in **C7**.

At **D** the remaining three saxes play pads for the alto, avoiding his pitches so that 4-part harmony results when the four saxes play together. Rather than use a turnaround at the end of this chorus, I have the bass and piano play a descending chromatic full cadence. This makes a dramatic break for the 4-bar interlude.

Interlude

The alto improvises over a chimes-like effect in the piano, followed by a little finger wagging in the now open brass. This humorous figure has its precedent in **A8**. It was swung in unison and played in plungers then, but now it is open, even 8ths and harmonized as a tonic C69.

[Let's listen to the intro and this chorus, **4-3: A-F**. Does it feel nice and relaxed, and of one piece, even though there are all kinds of changes in texture and orchestration?]

Melody Chorus #2, Vocal Quartet

This is the vocal quartet. There are no backgrounds other than the solo clarinet filigree—**All By Myself**, remember. The horns enter in the last bar of this chorus, **I8**, with the modulation. We are moving from C, Champian's key, to B♭, Denzal's key. Modulations are natural barriers. They establish the form. They give a lift to the arrangement.

Common Tone Modulation

The melody in the first trumpet is C, E♭, F (tonic and up the blues scale in C, and at the same time *re, fa, sol* in the new key of B♭). I scored this figure in 6-part harmony voiced in 3rds (five brass on top of the bari with the remaining saxes doubling brass notes and creating solid 3-part sax voicings at the same time). To get from C to A♭, I use Gm11 C7-9+5 B9+11. That takes us smoothly into the new key.

Rhythm, Rhythm and Rhythm—In that Order

All this melodic, harmonic and orchestrational stuff about the modulation is great, but what really makes it work is the rhythm of the figure. That was my initial idea. Next, I created the melody, then the harmony, and then the orchestration. The more central the modulating figure is to the arrangement, the more we buy the modulation. In this case I used a 3-note figure: 8th, quarter, 8th, starting on the second beat. It just felt natural when I wrote it, but now that I think of it, this figure is the second, third, and fourth notes of the melody, displaced by one beat. The melody starts with this rhythm on beats 3 and 4 of the first measure. The modulation does it a beat earlier in the bar—on beats 2 and 3. This 3-note version of the original motif will be central to the rest of this arrangement.

Melody Chorus #3, Solo Vocal

This is a solo vocal chorus for Denzal. Aside from the lift resulting from the modulation, the shift from 2 into 4 in the bass and drums gives tremendous forward motion and a more modern feel. All of a sudden we have gone from 1939 to 1959. That may not sound like much to someone born after 1980, but for a guy my age (born in 1949), the difference is monumental.

Honoring the Opposites

In this 3-chorus chart we have:

Chorus #1: Sax solo with harmonized horn answers and backgrounds.

Chorus #2: Harmonized vocal quartet with clarinet solo accompaniment.

Chorus #3: Vocal solo with more active horn answers and backgrounds.

Each chorus needs to be as different as possible from the previous chorus, or we lose interest. Opposite orchestration (brass/reeds), opposite texture (harmonized/solo or unison), vocal versus instrumental, and in the last chorus—modulating to a different key. Let's add choppy versus smooth. In this last chorus, I want Denzal to sing longer notes and smoother rhythms than the quartet did. He's a trained singer with a great sound; let's make use of that.

Call-and-Response

Notice that I used call-and-response in the first chorus with the alto solo. I avoid this convention in the second chorus to differentiate it from the first, so the clarinet plays throughout the chorus. I return to call-and-response in the third chorus. It feels really satisfying to begin by leaving Denzal two bars on his own, and then to have the horns play a strong 2-bar response. Letter **J** is brass vs. reeds, Letter **K1-7** is reeds, **K8** through letter **L** is *tutti*, **M** and **N** are brass vs. reeds, with the exception of **M5** and **N7-8**, which are *tutti*.

Orchestration and texture help to define the form.

Brass vs. Reeds and Reversal

Letter **J** consists of 8 bars divided up into four 2-bar blocks: vocal call responded to by unison brass over a harmonized sax pad, vocal call responded to by unison saxes with harmonized brass hits. Hence the brass and reeds

reverse their roles. In **J2-4** the saxes hold out a C9-5 chord in Drop 2 and then answer the brass with two 8th note chords (G♭7-5 to F7-5 in Drop 3 with the roots on the bottom).

The trumpets and trombones are in octaves playing an 8th note line that starts with a chromatic lower neighbor before ascending and descending diatonically, thus combining both the motif and counter-motif. Notice how the horns don't wait for the vocal to finish his opening phrase. This creates nice forward motion. It's like the old scenario where the husband, who hasn't quite finished his breakfast, is being pushed out the front door by his wife and told to go to work—because her lover is coming in by the back door.

In **J7-8** I reverse the sax and brass functions. The saxes play an octave unison line. Although I've used a chromatic turnaround in the brass and rhythm section, the saxes play a descending B♭ blues pentatonic lick that reflects the original B♭ chord change but with a ♭7, which implies the blues. The brass plays three off-beat upper structure triads before being joined by the saxes (F/D7, E♭/D♭7 and B♭/Cm7).

These first 5½ beats are opposite to **J2-4** in several ways:

1. The saxes and brass switch linear and harmonic roles.

2. The ascending brass unison line is replaced by a descending sax unison.

3. The smooth, sustained middle to low register pad in the saxes gives way to accented, high punctuations in the brass.

4. The separate, syncopated horn interruptions of the vocal line in the first phrase wait for the vocal to finish his second phrase before answering together after the downbeat.

Notice how the brass and saxes come together for the last 4 notes in the turnaround leading to letter **K**. They continue the Bb7 blues pentatonic implied by the saxes. The Ab is harmonized as the 13th of a B9 (rather than as the bland 7th of the Bb7 chord in the rhythm section), the F and Eb are left as unisons (integrating the sax unison and harmonized brass) and the final F is the 5th of an anticipated Bb69 chord voiced primarily in 4ths. The saxes merely double the bottom four of the five brass. This leaves the lead trumpet to his own pitches so that he can play with personality.

Bringing Down the Volume and Intensity

By omitting the brass and taking the sax dynamics down a level, the *b* section of the song at letter **K** creates a temporary relaxation, but all the while, we know that the return of the *a* section will bring back the brass at letter **L**. The saxes answer by moving back and forth between harmonized chords and unisons.

Superimposing Minor Triads

The vocal begins this section with a Dm arpeggio connected by a chromatic lower neighbor in the first measure and a diatonic and chromatic passing tone in the second measure before descending diatonically to the chromatic F# in **K4**. The saxes answer with a Cm displaced arpeggio. The G is the 3rd of Em7-5, the C is the respelled +9 of A7-9 and the Eb is the flat 5th of the same A7-9 chord. The first two voicings are in Drop 2, and the last voicing is in Drop 3 with the root on the bottom of the bass clef. Ending with a root position chord gives a feeling of cadence (finality).

Unisons with Chromatic Lower and Upper Neighbors

In **K4** and **K6** the sax unison answers to the vocal bring back the chromatic lower neigh-bors of our motif, but also do it one better by also adding upper neighbors. The upper neighbors are both chromatic and diatonic, being in the key and also a half-step above the target note (Bb to A in **K4** and Eb to D in **K6**). The sax pad comes back in **K5** as a 4-part close Gm7-5 chord.

Reversing the Neighbor Tone Function

The G at the end of **K6** resolves down to its chromatic lower neighbor on the downbeat of **K7**, giving us a surprise chromatic flat 5th on the Cm7-5. Then after arpeggiating up the Cm7-5 to the Eb, the line reverses directions and lands on the lower neighbor, D, which is the dissonant 9th of the Cm7-5 (a half step below the flat 3rd chord tone).

Tutti Call-and-Response

Letter **L** takes a different approach to call-and-response. The horn *tutti* begins a bar early (**K8**) utilizing the rhythm of the modulation figure of **I8** along with a lower neighbor (F# to G) and continues, thus reversing the call-and-response roles with the vocal. All the *tutti* voicings are 4-part close and doubled at the unison between saxes and brass in traditional manner. I used passing chords in the turn-around in **K8**: B9 C9 F13-9. The chromatic approach gives everyone the chromatic lower neighbor, which is so thematic.

Disguising the Symmetry of the Song

Although the 8-bar section of the song at letter **L** is made up of four 2-bar blocks, I've opted to reorganize the phrases over the original chord changes, so that we now have the asymmetrical 1+2+2+1+1+1. It still equals 8 bars, but the song changes hands where we don't expect it. This took a bit of recomposing from me—not only the horn parts, but also the vocal, since he now answers the horns. I kept the original words and developed the chromatics of our motif. In **L1** the horns play a chromatic lower neighbor on the *and* of 2 (A6 with an E in the melody) resolving back up to a B♭6, a B9+5 and B♭69.

The vocal answers with chromatic lower and upper neighbors (C# and E♭ circling the D) before resolving to a striking G to D♭ descending tritone in **L3**. I've re-harmonized that measure. Instead of C9, I use its tritone sub, G♭9, to make the D♭ melody feel consonant. That chord is preceded by its dominant, D♭9, of which the G melody is the flat 5th—spicy stuff.

Re-using the modulating rhythm, I stick with the G♭9 in **L4**, except for the chromatic C9 approach chord. In **L6-7** the vocal reverses direction and descends chromatically. I originally had another figure written in this bar for Denzal, but he improvised this chromatic phrase. It felt natural and I liked it better than what I had written, so we went with it. If something better comes along, I'm all for it. **L7** has the horns going back to the ascending chromatic idea. I alternated passing chords with D9's: D9 D⁰ D9 D9 E♭9 D9. The roots are omitted in the horns on the 9th chords.

Bringing it all Home

The vocal goes back to the original melody in **L8** while the horns rest, to clear our palates. I need a new texture for the last 8 bars of the song. So I give the saxes a thumb line and have the five brass players in 5-part harmony answer them and the vocal with a repetitive rhythm based on the vocal rhythm in **M1**. This happens two times on the rhythm of the middle three notes and then adding the fourth note on the *and* of 4. Chromatics abound. Notice that I avoid doubling pitches between the saxes, 1st Trumpet, bass, and vocal. The vo-

cal does touch upon a C in **M2** for a beat but quickly reverses direction, so that we don't confuse the trumpet and vocal lines.

After sufficient space in **M4**, the horns go to 5-part voicings with the saxes doubling the bottom four brass for one bar. Their figure answers the shape and rhythm of the vocal line from the previous measure, but inverted. The re-harmonization for this bar moves down chromatically: E♭13+11 Dm11 D♭13+11 C7+5+9 B9+11. The B9+11 is the tritone sub of the original chord from the song (the dominant, F7). Next the vocal answers with a 1-bar break, leading us into the coda.

Coda

The 8-bar coda is constructed 2+2+1+1+2. While Denzal holds out the tonic, the band alternates tonic/subdominant/tonic/subdominant/tonic. The ♭7 blue note on the *IV* chord (D♭) satisfies us in two ways:

1. It feels like the blues.
2. It's a half step lower than the 3rd of the tonic chord.

Each brass voice stays on his common-tone except for the 1st Trombone who, *all by himself,* slides down and up chromatically (just like our motif).

More Call-and-Response

The octave unison saxes answer the harmonized brass arpeggiating up an E♭13 chord, changing direction to slide down chromatically from the 7th to the 13th, and finally resolving to our happy note, G, the 6th of our tonic. These two bars repeat, but this time with a note added to the saxes to give some forward motion. The brass then repeats with added chromatics.

Pulling Out All the Stops

On the surface **M5** appears to be another repetition of the **M1** brass riff with the first trumpet reaching up to the flat 7th (A♭) for the last note, rather than repeating the 5th (F). I could have left it as repeated B♭69's resolving to an F7+9—but this is the spot in the arrangement where all the motifs and development get pulled together.

The first trumpet minor 3rd leap is the minor 3rd leap in the motif. The two trombones move down and up chromatically just like the first 3 notes of the motif. The bass moves down chromatically to the tritone sub of the dominant (B7 replacing F7). I have the saxes join the brass for the final B7 to give them more weight. The saxes are voiced below the brass, with the bari on the root. I used upper structure triads on three out of these five chords: F/E♭7, F/Dm7, E♭/D♭7, C7+9+5, D♭/B7.

The Final Motivic Statement

The density and rapid pace of these moving complex chords stuns us for a second, so I have the rhythm section break (rest) following this bar. This gives us a moment to digest what we have heard. It also challenges Denzal to answer with his final statement in **N6**. Since the brass lick ascends, as does the first statement of the title (our motif—**A1-4**, **F1-3**, and **J1-4**), I feel a need to counter that with a descending statement.

Also, the descending blues pentatonic in **N6** gives us a bit of a surprise ending. All along the music is cheerful, even though the lyrics are about loneliness. Our hero is trying to convince himself (and us) that he's okay, but in the end we find out that, under that mask, he is indeed lonely. The descending line and the blue 3rd do their job.

The Band Has the Last Word

After Denzal sings, "All by myself" for the last time in a descending B♭ blues pentatonic, the band answers with an opposite ascending C blues pentatonic (the retrograde of Denzal's line transposed up a step, answering his "All by myself" with *their* "All by myself."

The entire band is in octave unison for the first three notes and spreads out into 6-part harmony for the final tonic chord (B♭13+11). Using a dominant 7th for the final chord leaves us with the feeling of the blues. The trumpets have a C major upper structure triad over the 3rd and 7th in the bones. The saxes double the bottom three brass while the tenor fills in the missing 5th of the chord. This puts the saxes in 4-part close harmony voiced from the 9th down to the 3rd. All four band notes are syncopated. It's close to Denzal's rhythm, but just different enough not to sound too imitative.

Because the horns ascend and end on a tonic chord with a major 3rd, it's like they are saying, "Denzal, don't worry. Things will be okay." However, the flat 7th and flat 5th in the chord are blue notes, which say, "Well, maybe so, but it's not gonna be easy."

[Listen again to **4-1: Complete Arrangement**. See if it has enough variety (rhythm, melody, harmony, orchestration, and dynamics) to keep our interest without seeming disjunctive. I chose this song and this treatment because I wanted to create a comfortable piece that is easy to listen to, but not boring—like coming home and putting on a worn old pair of slippers and a soft robe, plopping down into your Morris chair... okay, you get the idea. See if all that comes across for you.]

Sheet music cover, 1919. Source: Arizona State University Digital Repository, ASU Sheet Music Collection

5. I Was So Young (You Were So Beautiful)

[At www.suchsweetthundermusic.com/pages/cjca2-accompanying-files listen to **5-1: Complete Arrangement.**]

This wistful 1919 ballad remembering the bittersweet ecstasy and pain of young love comes from a long-forgotten show entitled **Good Morning, Judge**. The music was composed by a 20-year-old George Gershwin with lyrics by Irving Caesar—a great example of what Duke Ellington used to call "a plaintive song." I was completely unaware of this gem until I heard Bill Charlap play it at Dizzy's, some 85 years after its creation. It was one of those moments when I say to myself, "This song is so beautiful. I can't believe I don't know it." It made me wonder how it escaped becoming a standard. Hopefully that mistake will be corrected in the near future.

Capturing the Mood Suggested By the Song

Bill's tasty arrangement (recorded on his **Bill Charlap Plays George Gershwin: The American Soul CD**) is reminiscent of the Bill Evans trio. My arrangement for vocalist Denzal Sinclaire takes a different approach. I'm not sure that I realized it when I wrote the chart, but listening to my arrangement now, I am reminded of Jimmie Lunceford's *Dream Of You,* which was composed, arranged and sung by Sy Oliver. Sy's intimate vocal and the slightly nostalgic clarinet sound perfectly capture the spirit of lost love. Denzal gives more of a Nat Cole approach to our recording, but, like Sy, I used four clarinets. The arrangement and performance are all about capturing the mood.

An Unusual Song Form

The unusual form of this song is a 12-bar verse followed by a 22-bar chorus. The chorus is made up of three sections: *a* (8 bars), *a'* (4 bars), *b* (10) bars. There are two sets of lyrics for the verse, one for a man to sing and one for a woman. I liked both so much that I had Denzal sing both. Before he sings the female verse he says, "You said." By using both verses, I could do intro, verse, chorus, verse, chorus, coda and have a complete 4-minute and 41-second track. I didn't want to break the mood and narrative by including an instrumental interlude or solo.

Paul's Comments on the Lyrics

Irving Caesar in 1930. Source: Wikipedia.

"**I Was So Young (You Were So Beautiful)** gives me a chance to say something about Irving Caesar, one of those important figures who somehow never gets his due. He was as fine a lyricist as anyone working during the period (late 1910s to mid-1940s). He embraced the demotic style of lyric that Irving Berlin popularized, though he was also capable of working in the flowery, self-consciously poetic style that operetta doted on.

Caesar's most famous lyric is almost certainly *Tea For Two,* from **No, No, Nanette**. That melody offered a wordsmith very little space in which to work. Caesar dashed off a dummy lyric, intending to replace it before opening night. Somehow, he never got around to it, and his off-the-top-of-his-head improvisation became as famous as any lyric ever written. Its perfectly crafted short phrases and naive sentiments are exactly right for the silly teens who sing them, and charmingly convey un-spoiled optimism about love. To achieve that so effortlessly bespeaks a great talent.

I Was So Young is an interesting transition-al song. The verse/chorus structure was the standard for ballads in the late nineteenth and early twentieth centuries. A classic example is *After The Ball* (which modern audiences know from **Show Boat**). Such songs had very lengthy verses that told the story, which the chorus then commented on. They were ballads indeed (in the sense of a story-in-song verse/chorus) and began to be replaced in the 1910s by the now-standard *aaba* format. While the new structure often still included an introduc-tory verse, it was not integral. The song could be enjoyed without it, and usually was. Today, verses have almost entirely disappeared.

I Was So Young combines the old-fashioned verse/chorus format with the direct, conver-sational language of the songs Berlin was making such a splash with. In that sense, it is quite innovative. If you listen to Gershwin's piano roll performance, there was more than a little ragtime still clinging to it, morphing into the twenties jazz style that he was the mas-ter and virtual inventor of. This brings out the transitional character of the piece even more clearly."

Let's start with the standard lead sheet.

(See *Example 5-1*, next page.) In the case of most standard songs, I can't be sure if the chord changes on the lead sheet or sheet mu-sic were the creation of the composer or an arranger working for the publisher. However this is not in question here, since Gershwin made a piano roll of himself playing the song.

Much as I respect Gershwin's songwriting, I don't feel obligated to copy his rhythms or harmonies literally; hence I've done quite a bit of re-harmonization to give the song more of the wistful quality that the music and lyrics suggest. The use of the *ivm* (the chord of sor-row) and the flat 9th on the dominants (which adds schmaltz) abound. The melody/bass re-lationship is primary, and once that had been established, the chord qualities (inside voices) easily fell into place.

Chord Qualities

When I was young, I used more dominant 7th chords because they were easy to voice lead, easy to improvise over, and afforded the most possibilities for tensions and altered tensions. I thought that other chord qualities sounded bland and lacked blues content. Not only did this proclivity for dominant chords produce a high degree of sameness in my music, but it also diminished my discovery of new sounds and combinations of sounds.

As time went on, I was naturally drawn to other kinds of chords that were suggested by melody/bass relationships. I still write bass lines that primarily move around the cycle of 5ths, or up or down by step (those are the strongest progressions); but more triads and non-tertian chords (built in 4ths and 5ths, symmetrical voicings etc.) have gradually crept into my music. I have also learned that "bland" chords can sound wonderful in the proper contexts.

LEAD SHEET

I WAS SO YOUNG
(You Were So Beautiful)

Gershwin/Caesar

I was a boy with a boy-ish heart Bow-ing down to love's com-mand.
You speak of love just as if you know what that won-drous pas - sion means.

You were a girl with a wo-man's art,__ and you held my fate in your hand.__
Heats that are young find a love that's new__ when they wake from fool__ ish dreams.__

I was the moth. You were the flame. You led me on.__ I was-n't to blame.
Poor lit - tle moth chas-ing the flame, I know you've told a - noth-er the same.

I was so young, you were so beau - ti-ful, what was a fel-low to do?

I was en-rap-tured with you. They told me not to, but still I loved you, how I loved you.

I was so young, you were so beau - ti-ful, I knew you could n't be true.__

© 2010 Such Sweet Thunder

Example 5-1: Lead sheet.

Intro

After re-harmonizing the verse and chorus of this song, I had a pretty good idea of how I wanted to arrange it—enough so, in fact, that I got out my score paper and began with the intro. As I've said before, I normally start writing at letter **A** and leave an empty page for my intro, which I will come back to write when I know where the chart is going. That was not the case here. Right from the start, I knew the mood, and that I would be using 4 clarinets, 3 trombones and an independent solo baritone sax. The piano would be used prominently accompanying the vocal on the verses—hence his preview in the intro. Notice how he is *tacet* during the choruses. This gives the piece clarity, contrasting sections, and draws our attention to the piano all the more to when he does play.

A Buddy Rich Story

The trumpets are used sparingly and, although I carry four in my band, I only need three for this arrangement. If I used a fourth, he would only be doubling trombone notes. I generally like to avoid doubling pitches when writing for the brass section. I don't know how trombonists feel, but doubling a trombone and a trumpet at the unison feels unpleasant for the trumpet player. It's not a natural blend, since the trombone is in a much stronger register of his instrument.

This reminds me of when I was arranging for Buddy Rich's band 40 years ago. I wrote a chart that had a tenor battle in the middle. Buddy said that it needed backgrounds for the soloists. His exact words were, "I'm paying 14 men; I want them all to play."

Although this sort of thinking may have some merit in the business world, it's not always the best course in the arts. I normally do involve everyone in the climax of an arrangement, but even then, there might be exceptions.

The finish to this story is that I told Buddy that I preferred no backgrounds for this chart, so he said that he would make some up, and that I wouldn't like them. He was right—I didn't like them. He opened his show every night for the next two years with that chart (using his backgrounds).

Starting with a Melodic Fragment

When I was a kid in summer camp, immediately following lunch we would clear the plates off the tables and then Manny, the owner of the camp, would enthusiastically lead us in a group sing—folk songs, Broadway songs from the Golden Era, camp songs, etc. My buddy, Pete, who was a couple of years older than me, would accompany us on piano. He had a standard intro—he would play the last 4 bars of the song. It always worked.

It doesn't give away the beginning of the song, but it gives the singer(s) and the listeners enough information so that, when letter **A** comes, everyone is comfortable. The key is established, as well as the tempo, style, mood, dynamics, and melodic motif. An artistic plus is that it's going to be 28 bars before we hear that part of the melody again. By that time we'll have practically forgotten those **4** bars, but they remain in our subconscious.

Over the years I've used Pete's formula—actually it is a very common and useful technique for creating intros, but it always reminds me of my old friend, and how we used to laugh so hard that our sides would ache.

One variation on Pete's technique is to start with a melodic fragment, rather than stating two, four or eight measures of the melody. In **I Was So Young (You Were So Beautiful)**, I start the intro with the clarinet playing the melody of the first 3 beats of measure **D7**. I've altered the rhythm, so that the quarter note triplet will float. We won't know until the third bar of the intro if we are in 3/4 or 4/4 time. I like this ambiguity. It grabs my attention and piques my interest, so that I want to

keep listening. Also, alluding to waltz-time creates a nostalgic feeling, which is key to this song and arrangement.

Our Central Motif and its Opposite

The central motif for the chorus of this song is the first measure of the melody (**B1**)—G, A♭, B♭, B♭ *(mi, fa, sol, sol)*. Interval-wise, it's an ascending minor 2nd, an ascending major 2nd and a repeated note. Gershwin develops this motif mostly by sequencing it a step lower (F, G, A♭, A♭) and inverting it. He pretty much stays with diatonic sequencing but uses passing chromatics as lower neighbors (**B5**) or to connect ideas (**C4**, **C7** and **C8**).

Much in the same way that bridges to songs should appear to be the opposite of the *a* sections, verses should also appear on the surface to be the opposite of the chorus. It is imperative for the arrangement to prove the oneness of the verse and chorus.

The verse to this song begins with a descending chromatic scale fragment from the 5th of E♭ major down to the 3rd, which is the opposite of the ascending diatonic fragment of our central motif. Both the motif and counter-motif travel between the 3rd and 5th of E♭. Not only does one descend and one ascend, but also, one moves chromatically and one diatonically. Additionally, our motif has a repeated note, while our counter-motif continues downward diatonically until it settles on a long note (C). The C is repeated to begin the next phrase.

If we eliminate the F in **A2** and the G in **A4**, these first 4 bars of the verse descend an octave from B♭ down to B♭—first chromatically and then diatonically. The twice-repeated C, B♭ descending whole step, will be inverted in **D7** to be the two ascending whole steps (C to

D and B♭ to C). This youngster Gershwin has got some potential, don't you think?

The First Measure of a Chart

Ideally, the first bar we hear should tell us the whole story of the piece. It's like how the DNA from just one of your cells defines your entire body. It should also be subtle. You don't want to hit your listener over the head with how clever you are. Measure **1** has the clarinet playing two sets of whole steps while the clarinet just under him moves up and down chromatically and the other two clarinets descend by half step. So we have the ascending diatonic whole steps of our motif, and the descending half step of our counter-motif. And one more thing—the initial C in the melody is repeated at the end of the measure, which alludes to the repetition of the third note of our motif.

The second measure of the chart is a variation of the first. The baritone sax plays two whole steps in the same rhythm as the top clarinet of bar **1**, except that the bari continues upward with his second set of 2nds. The three chromatic clarinets are replaced by three trombones performing a similar function.

Measure **3** has the piano rhapsodizing. His right hand plays inverted major 2nds while the left hand plays a series of chromatically descending 9th chords (a technique of Willie "The Lion" Smith that he passed on to his two disciples—George Gershwin and Duke Ellington. Measure **4** introduces repeated G's in the right hand but resolves first to C and then to B♭ (our inverted major 2nd).

When I wrote this intro, I was completely unaware of its relationship to the motifs of the song. In fact, it wasn't until I wrote this chapter that I even thought about any of this. My preparation for writing this chart was playing the song over and over with the intent of finding tempo, melodic phrasing and suitable harmonies. I didn't give any thought to the intro. I improvised it, and wrote it down on the score paper. Having learned the song, my subconscious mixed it all up, and spat out this intro—much in the same manner that my daily life gets processed in my dreams.

Re-composing on the Spot

When we first read the chart down at the recording session, I immediately realized that I wanted the piano to be more expressive, so I had him play his two bars *rubato*. This adds another dimension to the intro and makes the *a tempo* at **A** all the more effective. I originally had the bass playing descending quarter note roots below the piano, but with the piano now being rubato, it is more effective to wait for the bass and drums to establish the time at letter **A**.

Verse One

The vocal enters at **A** along with the bass and drums. The cup-muted trombones play mostly triadic ascending pyramids. The unison clarinets start with descending major 2nds before expanding to a full diatonic pattern. Note the rhythmic overlapping of the lead trombone and the clarinets. They play the second beat of the bar together. The clarinets are above the bone and play a descending 8th note on 2 *and*. I was careful to keep the clarinets off Denzal's pitches. The texture is a modern, chromatic variation of Classical melody/accompaniment figures found in Haydn and Mozart. The rhythm is generated by the pointillism of having different musicians play on all eight 8th notes of each bar.

A5-6 is identical to **A1-2** (with different words), so I repeated this interesting pattern and continued it for another measure, slightly varying the first trombone. **A8** cadences on the tonic. I reused the ♭*II* to *I* cadence (Emaj7 E♭6) that I introduced in **A4-5**.

Charleston/Pedal Point

At **A9** the horns rest to clear our palate, and the piano returns. Suddenly the rhythm section becomes a more integral part of the arrangement. The piano and drums play Charleston rhythms while the bass answers the vocal. The original chord change on the third beat of bar **A9** is C7. That felt too defined to me. I wanted the music to float here—like the moth in the lyric. The G diminished chord is the top part of a C7-9. Instead of moving to a C in the bass, I keep the F from the previous Fm7. This somewhat unusual Gº/F sounds perfectly natural, since the F in the bass is held over and eventually resolves up a 4th to B♭. The final *fermata* in **A12** gracefully leads us into the chorus.

Differentiating the Verse and Chorus

It's usually a good idea to differentiate the verse from the chorus—in much the same way

Verse	Chorus
First 8 bars Trombone pyramids Unison clarinet 8th notes	Concerted bone voicings w/bari solo line alternating with no voicings Unison clarinet thumb line in half notes and quarters
Last 4 bars Rhythm section Pedal Point *Fermata* (out of tempo)	Piano *tacet/* Unison clarinets Diatonic/chromatic bass movement In tempo

that we differentiate the bridge from the main section of a song, or the intro from the song. Changing rhythm, melody, harmony and orchestration is often not enough. We are so accustomed to hearing the verse out-of-tempo and the chorus in tempo, that it has become almost *de rigueur*. The *fermata* will take care of this.

Chorus

In order for the listener to understand the form, the chorus must appear to be opposite in most ways from the verse, but still retain some elements, so that both sections feel like they are part of the same piece. This is a tricky balance. The elements in play are shown in the table below.

Less is More

For me the two most striking differences are the *a tempo* in **B1** following the *fermata* in **A12**, and the unaccompanied clarinet thumb line in **B1-3**. The nakedness of not having trombone pyramids or pads playing voicings is at first startling, but then it pushes us to focus on the melodic lines in play: vocal, clarinet and bass. When the bones and bari enter in **B4**, the effect is very comforting. Pads make us feel secure. Repeating this texture (but with a more active clarinet line) in **B6-7** makes us feel that we are getting our money's worth from this texture. When I discover something really good, I want it to come back. It gives the piece unity, and it feels satisfying to take that second or third bite.

Trombone Pads

For the most part, I avoid the vocal melody notes in the bone voicings. This gives us two distinctive personalities. In **B4-6** none of the bone notes double the vocal. The same goes for the baritone sax line. In **B4-6**, the only bari/vocal doubled note is the C on the downbeat of **B6**. Those notes arrive by contrary motion, making this temporary agreement desirable. The vocal descends while the bari ascends. Also notice that the bari does not double any of the bone notes. This is key to my lean style of writing. Doubling diminishes individuality, personality and color. The essence of art is conflict and resolution.

The sharper the disagreement, the more satisfying the resolution.

Re-introducing Elements

After a while, it can be effective to re-introduce previous elements.

This happens with the 8th notes in the clarinets in **B6** and the contrapuntal bone writing in **B8**. I just give you a taste though, and then it's back to the same material we had in **B1-2** for **C1-2**. The melody repeats, so why not have everyone repeat? If I can repeat an idea, I will. If it doesn't feel right to me, I'll change it or create something new.

Repetition leads to the establishment and recognition of character. However, too much repetition results in predictability.

More Trombone Pads

The bones have two measures of rest at letter **C**, which is just enough time to grab their plungers. You always need to choreograph the application of mutes, the change of instruments, grabbing the bow, etc. in tempo to be sure that it can not only be done in time, but that it will be comfortable enough for the player to enter on the next phrase solidly.

At this slow tempo, two bars is plenty of time. For quick changes, brass players will usually place upcoming mutes on their stand either at the top of the chart or during a long rest. In this case, I originally had the bones play open for letter **C**, but that sounded too obtrusive, too "in my face." The plungers make them sound more distant and sexier. Notice how the vocal and three bones combine to make 4-part harmony. In most cases the bass note is not doubled in the bones or vocal, so we now have 5-part harmony with the bassist.

Emotional Meaning in Chord Qualities

The bone entrance in **C3** is a nice surprise. The +9 in the lead trombone gives the illusion of moaning. Combined with the sexuality of the plungers and the accent our guys put on their entrance, we have a startling wake-up call. The next measure softens the blow. The sophisticated 9th chord with the +11 followed by the sentimental -9 and the seduction of the +5 all serve to soften the blow and keep us in the romantic game. The girl in the song is manipulating us, and we are too weak to resist. By the way, count up all the *ivm* (A♭m) chords in this chart. *ivm* is the chord of despair. You know this affair isn't going to end well.

Smooth vs. Choppy

The bones alternate between smooth and choppy in this chart. We first hear them play smoothly in the second bar of the intro, but then they switch to choppy in their pyramids at **A**. Their rhythmic figures (mostly syncopated) at **B** are choppy. They are back to smooth from **C3-D3**. The short downbeat and syncopation in **D4** give us a taste of choppy before reverting a bar later to smooth half notes. **D6-10** is all choppy, due to the Charleston syncopations. Even **D10** is a Charleston, albeit displaced by an 8th note.

I finally introduce the trumpets in **D6**. They are in hats and join the bones for four bars.

Since recording this chart, I have had second thoughts, and for future performances I plan to have the trumpets *tacet* their notes in **D6** and enter a bar later. My reasoning is that I find that the trumpet figures in **D6** confuse this already complicated form. If they enter a bar later, they confirm the form.

Second Verse

Reversing the orchestration of the first verse, we have just the voice and piano *rubato* for 8 bars, before the horns and rhythm section play the final four bars in time. When the horns enter, it is the brass in cups playing Charlestons with answers from the bari sax. The 6-part brass voicings use mostly upper structure triads in the trumpets. The richness is in contrast to all the previous textures in this chart.

Second Chorus and Coda

The *D.S.* covers the first 20 bars of the chorus before moving on to the coda. Denzal stretches out his last word—truly savoring "beautiful." The clarinets get their last licks answering him. This line synthesizes the verse and chorus and lands on a surprise E69 with the blue note (G♭) on top and a second blue note (D♭)

right under. This is my favorite moment in the chart. The clarinets sound so vulnerable.

Final Brass and Bari Sax Statements

The brass make their final statement also compounding the verse and chorus motifs, but, whereas the clarinets are diatonic until their last two notes, the brass concentrate more on the chromatics of the verse, first inverted to an ascending line before descending chromatically into the final cadence. The baritone sax gets his last licks in by holding out a dominant pedal throughout the chromatic brass chords.

Coming to Agreement

The beautiful dissonance of the final E13+11 to E♭13+11 with the 13ths in the melody connote the bittersweet feeling of the blues. The only time that all the horns play together is on the last two chords. Finally we agree: lost love is both beautiful and painful.

[Let's listen again to **5-1: Complete Arrangement**. There is so much repetition in so few score pages. How do we stand on sameness and difference? Is there enough surprise, or do things become predictable? Does it tell the story? Do we feel Denzal's pain? His loss? His ambivalence?]

6. No Sign Of You

[At www.suchsweetthundermusic.com/pages/cjca2-accompanying-files listen to **6-1: Complete Arrangement.**]

This song has an interesting history. I originally composed **No Sign Of You** for a musical that never got produced. It sat in my piano bench and then in a box on one of my shelves for 25 years. I had composed seven songs for that show. The lyrics and book didn't work, but I thought the music should have a life at some point. When Paul and I discussed writing songs reminiscent of our favorite songwriters for a recording project, I played him this tune. He immediately liked it and sent me a set of lyrics the next day. Perhaps because of the minor key and 1920s setting of the show, this song has always reminded me of Cole Porter and, due to its chromaticism, it seemed ripe for a more modern arrangement.

I never mentioned the original title or lyrics that had inspired my melody to Paul, since they were irrelevant at this point, and he came up with a completely different story. We did a little polishing on the lyric over the next couple of days. If I remember correctly, he wrote either an additional chorus or an extra bridge, which seemed unnecessary—one chorus and a tag ending is plenty. I don't think we changed my melody at all, although that does sometimes happen in the course of justifying the music and lyrics—just as the U.S. House and Senate are supposed to do when they can agree enough to enact laws—a little dark political humor there.

When Paul and I wrote book shows, the lyrics almost always came first. Songs in shows are so plot- and character-driven that the lyrics are much too specific to try to fit them to music. Some of our stand-alone songs follow the same routine, but for the great majority, the music came first. I am equally happy working either way. Whoever comes up with a good idea first gets the attention of the other. If my melody doesn't inspire a lyric, I stick it in my trunk and write another.

We had a few songs that were rewritten once or twice, and a few others that were abandoned. In the course of writing shows, we occasionally had to cut a really good song because it didn't fit in the action, and we couldn't find a spot for it. Sometimes a song just doesn't suit the character of the person singing it or their role in the show. As they say in the theater, if you want to have a successful show, you have to be willing to kill your babies.

This goes for arrangements of all types—instrumentals and vocals. The main focus has to be on the big picture. So often arrangers get hung up on hip techniques, voicings, etc., and lose sight of the audience's relationship to the story.

Songs from discarded shows and songs discarded from shows are called trunk songs. It's not uncommon for composers to pull old unused songs out of their "trunk" when they are stuck for a new song. There are a number of famous examples. One that comes to mind is Arthur Schwartz's *You And The Night And The*

Music, which he originally wrote for a revue in summer camp as a teenager.

My composition teacher, Ms. Ulehla, told me to *never* throw any music out—you never know when you'll be able to figure out how to make it work, and at some point, it could be just what you need.

My concept for this arrangement was to create a band accompaniment that would be wild and challenge the melody, since the melody is so smooth and relaxed. I wanted to evoke a feeling of danger. It's a sort of detective story. The minor key gives the song an ominous flavor.

Because of the long form (64 bars), the tempo needs to be fast in order to play a chorus within a minute or so. The form of this song is *aaba* (16 bars each with each of those sections made up of two 8-bar phrases). The form of the chart is Intro, Melody Chorus, Solo Chorus (split between trombone and clarinet), Recapitulation (½ chorus Melody starting at the bridge), and Coda. Very often a half chorus is sufficient for the recap, especially on long forms. No need to overstay your welcome.

The "Rules of Songwriting"

When I was a student I read all sorts of books on songwriting and got advice from teachers and other musicians. Two rules kept coming up:

1. The melodic range should not be more than a 10th from the lowest note to the highest note.
2. The highest note should only appear once, and that appearance should be ⅔ to ¾ of the way through the song.

I've pretty much stuck to this advice. A larger range limits who can sing your song and the choice of keys. On rare occasions I have expanded by a half step from a 10th to an 11th. In these cases, the bottom notes are not stressed, so they don't require much tone. Mostly my peak pitches have conformed to these two rules but, as we saw in *A Perfect Day*, the rules are not hard-and-fast. Some variation is possible.

I tend to regard rules as how things usually happen. If I have a good reason to do something different, I'm going to go with it.

The range of **No Sign Of You** (see *Example 6-1*, next page) is a minor 10th, from the tonic up to the minor 3rd a 10th above. The lowest pitch is the tonic, and it is the first note of the song. It appears a whopping 14 times. That's an awful lot, and on the surface it seems like it might be too much, but when I play the song or listen to it, it sounds just right to me.

Duke Ellington's rule: "If it sounds good, it is good."

This is a very diatonic tune—there are few accidentals and no wide or awkward intervals, so it should be fairly easy to sing.

The melody rises from the tonic up a 9th to B in **A7**. B reoccurs in the bridge at **C5** and **D3**. The peak note C appears in the next bar (**D4**). This conforms to the "rule." On the recap we get the high C in the same place in the bridge, but then we need a climax in the tag, so we repeat the high C in **R3**. It might have been nice to exceed the C, but C sounds right to me, especially since the previous C's were just touched on and are really just auxiliary pitches. *Example 6-2* is a lead sheet with the basic pitches marked with x's.

NO SIGN OF YOU

Words by Paul Mendenhall
Music by David Berger

Example 6-1: Lead sheet

NO SIGN OF YOU

Words by Paul Mendenhall
Music by David Berger

Example 6-2 Lead sheet with x's on basic pitches

This is how I hear the structure of this song. Let me explain. In general, I try to organize my thoughts in terms of priority. I deal with the most important things and then let the details fill themselves in. I use this method in just about everything in my life, not just music. I work from the largest concept to the smallest detail. Some people get hung up in details and lose sight of the big picture.

And so it is when I write music. My goal is to get to the end of the piece in a satisfying way. Everything else is subservient. Working backwards assures that the arrival points will feel satisfying. It doesn't matter where you came from, as long as you arrive smoothly at your destinations.

Auxiliary Pitches

When I composed this song, I wrote the entire melody and then made a few changes in the auxiliary pitches, but left the anchor pitches in place. The *a* section of this tune is 16 measures, consisting of two 8-measure phrases, both of which consist of two 4-measure phrases. Let's look at the four 4-measure phrases. The first two are quite similar (they share the same first four notes. Let's call these four bars *motif 1*. The first phrase continues descending to D, while the second phrase ascends to B. Both phrases are syncopated and move stepwise with small leaps of diatonic 3rds.

The third phrase is a contrast both in rhythm and shape—it consists of half notes in descending diatonic 5ths and ascending diatonic 4ths. Let's call this *motif 2*. Phrase four introduces the chromatic lower neighbor before returning to the syncopation of *motif 1*, thus

unifying the entire 16-bar a section. Let's call this phrase *motif 3*. The entire piece grows out of these three motifs (**Example 6-3**).

Our 16-bar bridge (letters **C** and **D**) consists of two 8-bar phrases where upper and lower neighbors (both diatonic and chromatic abound). **C1** has the same rhythm and shape as *motif 3* (with the slight alteration of a diatonic lower neighbor rather than the chromatic D#). **C2** continues the quarter note pace, but with a chromatic incomplete upper neighbor. **C3** is identical to *motif 1*, but is followed by the 3-quarter-note rhythm of *motif 3*. **C5-6** is identical to **A7-8**. I love when material comes back in a different measure of the form. This upsets the symmetry in a gentle way. We then come to rest on an F#, which is an interesting chromatic. From here we need to find our way home to A minor.

The second phrase of the bridge starts much like the first, only we are in C# minor (a step higher in the scale) and the order of neighboring tones is reversed to chromatic and then diatonic. **D3** returns to the half notes of **B**, except the pitches repeat rather than go around the cycle of 5ths. The same pattern repeats a 5th below in **D5-6** before we return to the half

Example 6-3

note pattern (this time in a descending blues scale segment—5, ♭5, 4, ♭3). Although letter **D** is an 8-bar phrase, it is constructed in a 2+4+2 design—again messing gently with the symmetry. After all this complicated chromatic and structural detail it's comforting to repeat the a section verbatim at **E** and **F**.

Adding a Bass Line

It felt right to me to start simply: *i vi7-5 ii7-5 V* for the first 4 bars. The second 4 bars have to get us to a B7 (the dominant of E), so that I can supply the missing harmony note between the 5ths in **B1-4**. The use of inversions gives this a bit of a restrained "Classical" feel. I like that change of character. We are down and dirty at **A**, and then nice and polite at **B**.

The sophistication of the chromatic bridge demands harmonies that go from C minor to C major to F# minor to C# minor to A major to A minor, ending with a chromatic turnaround back to A minor.

Adding Harmony

Finally, I determined what the chords were. Mostly the bass notes became the roots of the chords. I then filled in the inside voices with mostly diatonic notes. Chromatics were added for spice.

I once asked Bob Brookmeyer what he thought about while he was writing. He said simply, "Tension and release." Those opposites are always in my mind somewhere as well. It's mostly just a feeling—intuitive. I often like to do the opposite of what most people would expect—often making the consonant note the tension and the dissonant note the release.

My first choice for adding inside voices is to use diatonic notes. If that makes good sounding horizontal lines and vertical structures,

I'm done. Sometimes this can sound bland. If that is the case, I'll look for some chromatic alterations. It doesn't have to be much. I let the outer parts (melody and bass) set the tone.

Paul's Comments on Adding Lyrics

"When I heard this music, I immediately realized it called for a Cole Porter-style lyric, something smart and sophisticated. It was clear that the title needed to fall on the last phrase of each *a* section, as the music repeated at those points. The title popped into my head in response to that *da DA da DA* phrase.

The idea of searching was suggested by the title, and what kind of searching would be interesting? Clearly not an Internet search! So I thought of all the occult ways of locating someone: Ouija, tarot, crystal balls, etc. From there it was just a matter of working out the details.

You can't evoke Cole Porter without a clever rhyme or two, and I hit on one I particularly like: 'psychics' and 'my kicks.' It is always fun to find a rhyme that pairs two words with one. And then comes a pretty decent joke, playing with two meanings of 'kick:' 'That kind of kick only leaves a bruise.'

I like this song a lot. It has a jazzy, Rat-pack feel that makes me smile."

Intro

My concept is for this arrangement to be an exciting up-tempo barnburner. The intro is call-and-response with the drums—first band unison, and then harmonized reeds. The band unison is in their comfortable middle registers and only uses three different pitches: A, D and C. These are three of the five pitches in the opening motif. I've left out the B and the E and whittled down this motif to its core. My objective in the intro is to tell enough of the story to hook my audience, but not so much of the story as to give away the surprises. Think of movie trailers.

In this intro, the opening two measures give us the feeling for the entire piece. Now that I think of it, I could almost omit the next 6 bars and go directly to letter **A**. This could work, but I like shifting the orchestration. This sets up the idea of searching, which is what the lyric is all about.

There is another kind of shifting at the heart of this arrangement. The melody suggests a 2 feel with occasional moments in 1. There are lots of quarter notes, half notes and whole notes—no 8ths. The syncopations are either quarter-half-quarter or half-dotted whole note (augmentation of the first syncopation). These two kinds of syncopations initially appear in the first four measures of the song.

Intuitively, I picked up on the shifting gears and gave the horns some figures in 4. This happens right away in the intro. This sophisticated relationship of meters is developed throughout the arrangement. Different meters exist vertically (vocal in 2 while the rhythm section is in 4) and horizontally (vocal in 2 answered by brass in 4 or reeds in 1). When the vocal enters in 2 at **A**, we are surprised, following the 4 feel of the intro.

5-Part Rootless Voicings in the Reeds

The reed section response in bars **5-6** of the intro repeats the rhythm and melody of the opening phrase, but in addition to a change in orchestration (from *tutti* to the reeds), there is also a change in texture (from unison to thickened line harmonization). I've got Dan Block on clarinet throughout this chart, rather than his usual tenor saxophone. This not only gives me greater range, but a more exotic flavor.

The melody is in the clarinet at the top of the treble clef. I'm going to harmonize this line in 5-part voicings from the top down. For the most part I will not be concerned with using roots in the voicings. If they happen and sound good, okay. If not, I won't miss them, as long as the bass establishes them, and the bari part makes melodic sense and relates well to the other parts.

Repeating Voicings Where Melody Notes Repeat

A technique I sometimes employ to create continuity is to use the same chords and voicings whenever a pitch comes back. In this case, all the E's in the melody are voiced as Bm11-5, all the A's are voiced as Am69, and all the G's are voiced as E7+9+5. If the flavor of this chart wasn't apparent in the first two measures, these reed voicings let us know that we are exploring Ellingtonian minor key territory. I'm not trying to imitate any particular Ellington piece or sounds, but his wild charts on such minor key tunes like *It Don't Mean A Thing* and *Chocolate Shake* are so imbedded in my mind, that they've got me thinking in a certain vein.

Melody Chorus

We've got a 16-bar a section that repeats. I'm going to give the accompaniment to the brass the first time and the reeds the second. This will create enough contrast so that we won't become bored or complacent with the 16-bar repeat of the melody and chord changes. In addition to a change in orchestration, I'm going to give the brass and saxes different textures, different meters and different functions; call-and-response, thumb lines, pads, etc.

Brass in Plungers

The first time through **A** and **B**, I employ call-and-response between the vocal and the brass. To give the brass a more vocal and mocking sound, I have them play in plungers alternating between closed and open. This is instantly recognizable as an homage to Ellington's *It Don't Mean A Thing (if it ain't got that swing)*. The seven brass are harmonized in 5-part close voicings for the most part with the bottom two trombones doubling the top two trumpets down the octave. Some variations in the voicing scheme occur in order to make each brass part a good melody that combines well with the other brass and the bass. The half steps and major 7th intervals give the brass more spice and rhythmic punch.

To distinguish the brass from the vocal, I give them different implied meters (quarters and 8ths rather than halves and quarters). The vocal floats over the fast tempo implying half time, while the brass are playing syncopations in fast 4/4 tempo. I also avoid the vocal melody note in the top brass part. This establishes independence.

The basis of good counterpoint is assigning different rhythms and pitches to the different voices. Different colors, textures, registers and instrumentation can also help.

Let's look at the brass voicings. The first figure (**A4**) has four repeated voicings. The second figure (**A7-8**) has six notes and is a simplified version of the intro figure. As I did with the reeds in the intro, every time a melody note came back, I used the same voicing as its previous occurrence. So every A is voiced as an

F#m11-5, every D is a C13 and the final C is B7+5-9+9.

The bones play whole note bass notes in **B1-4** before the brass switch teams in **B4-5** and play a half-time syncopation. I omitted the lead trombone because I couldn't hear an additional pitch for him. I wanted this B7 voicing to sound more dissonant. Adding another pitch, or doubling a pitch at the octave would add some density, but at the same time diminish the dissonance. Notice the contrary and oblique motion when the B7+5+9-9 resolves to the Am69/E.

Earning the Cliché

The fourth brass figure (**B7-8**) is the cliché from *It Don't Mean A Thing*. What makes it work here is that it is a development of the brass figure in **A4**, which comes from a diminution of *motif 1*. So, because we have earned it, our cliché makes us feel satisfied, rather than cheated with something cheap and superficial.

Sax Thumb Line

The opposite of the brass harmonized call-and-response is a unison sax thumb line. The brass moved at twice the speed of the vocal. Now the saxes will move primarily at half the speed of the vocal. Again, to create good counterpoint, I will avoid the vocal melody notes in the sax line as well as the roots (which are covered by the bass). When the bass is playing an inversion (like Am/G in measure **A6**), I use the A root in the saxes and avoid the G, which is what the bass is playing.

A4 cried out for some movement, so I gave the saxes a simple moving line in ascending quarter notes that turns out to be the same pitches as the main motif of the song (A, B, C, E) but sequenced a diatonic step lower (G#, A, B, C). Until the moment of writing this last sentence, I was unaware of the motivic reference. When I wrote this figure, I was merely thinking that I was on an E7 and I needed to go from the G# up to a C in the next measure.

The sax counterpoint in **A5-6** moves in half time like the vocal, and comes to a unison B on the third beat of **A5**, but still sounds like two independent parts. Here's why: the syncopations in the vocal move against the half notes in the saxes, and the contrary motion between the ascending voice and descending saxes justifies the temporary unison B. Note also that the sax pitches in **A5-8** are the same as the vocal in **A1-4** except in a different order and the final note in the saxes is a controversial D#, rather than the plain D♮ in the vocal in **A4**. That D# must resolve at some point.

Changing Texture to Define the Form

The reeds (now with the clarinet on top) continue playing at half the tempo of the vocal, but change texture from unison to 5-part Drop 2 harmony. Played with no vibrato, these first five bars of letter **B** sound relaxed and cool (as opposed to the hot and agitated harmonized brass). The saxes return to unison in **B7-8** with a responsive 8th note lick that comes out of the intro figure. It's as if the saxes have been holding back for 14 bars, and finally get a chance to answer the voice with a zinger.

Continuing the Counterpoint In the Piano

When the voice moves to quarter notes on the bridge, the piano improvises at twice the speed—an 8th note bebop line. Never mind that the voice goes to long notes in **C5-8**. The piano continues at his hectic pace. In order to help the listener understand the structure of

the bridge, at **D**, I have the bones play 3-note voicings—one voicing per chord change. Each voicing avoids the vocal melody notes and in many cases also the bass note.

A Startling Turnaround

In a complete reversal of my contrapuntal approach to accompanying singers, I have the voice, reeds, bass and drums play the 3-note turnaround in **D7-8** together. This was done to give rhythmic emphasis to those three notes and to define the form—a signal that we are now returning to the *a* section of the song. I wouldn't use this technique over a long phrase, but it seems to work well in grabbing our attention and emphasizing these three crucial notes that help us to grasp the form.

Orchestrating the Final *a* Section

Very often *aaba* song forms use the same orchestration for all three *a* sections. This gives a chart cohesion. I do this when it feels right. I wanted this chart to be more challenging to the singer, band, listeners and myself. After all, the lyric is about searching here and there.

Each *a* section has the same melody and harmony, but is orchestrated in a vastly different way. We had plunger brass and then a unison sax thumb line. Now I need to come up with something different. **E1** is 4-part close saxes playing a basic syncopated figure. Although the bassist goes from an Am to an F#m7-5, the sax voicing stays on the same four pitches. Am6 and F#m7-5 differ only in the bass, so there is no need to change the voicing. The interesting thing here is the change in rhythmic gears in the saxes. Although the bassist has been walking in 4, the vocal is in 2 and the horns have been in 1. Now, all of a sudden, the sax syncopation implies that we are indeed in 4.

Voicing Considerations: Texture, Weight, and Dissonance

The ensemble figure in **E3-4** is also syncopated, and in 4. Since this is a rhythmic (as opposed to melodic) figure, and I'm looking for power and weight, I voice this out with the saxes under the brass in 5-part harmony. First I voiced the brass with the bones tight below the trumpets. Then I put the bari downstairs on the roots and voiced the other three saxes above him, making complete voicings in the saxes.

I omitted the clarinet, since he would only be heard if I put him above the lead trumpet; not a color I was looking for here. I also omitted the fourth trumpet because I wanted to keep the octave doubling in the brass to a minimum. I'm not concerned with unisons between the brass and saxes. This is unavoidable to a certain extent, and not disturbing to the players nor to the listeners. Each voicing has a tension added: Bm11-5, E7+9 and Am69. I also altered the 5th on the E7+9, making it E7+5-9.

Ascending Scalar Cliché

Measure **E7** is that overused cliché: an ascending scale leading to a break on the downbeat of the next bar. I gave the trumpets the normal ascending scale pattern, but employed contrary motion for the saxes. Due to the fast tempo, I omitted the bones on the run, and had them join on the downbeat of **E8** for punctuation.

I didn't notate a crescendo for the trumpets, since they normally crescendo while ascending. I don't need to tell them what they already know. I think it would feel unnatural for the saxes to crescendo while descending, so I didn't give them a dynamic marking. The

voicings that result from the horn lines are: F#m7-5, F°, F#m7-5, F#m7-5, Gm7-5, F#m7-5, B7+9+11.

Subito 18th Century Counterpoint

The inversions in the harmonies for the next 4 bars have always sounded more like Mozart to me than jazz, so I'm going to go in that direction—omit the rhythm section and write 4-part traditional species counterpoint. The third trombone moves pretty much in half notes with the voice (both use different pitches), while the bari is in whole notes (twice as slow) and the 2nd Alto is in quarter notes (twice as fast). It is essential that everyone gets a good melody, and that each melody sounds good against each of the others. What keeps this passage sounding like (or sorta like) jazz is the orchestration. The color and inflections of the two saxes could never be confused with Mozart.

The danger with abrupt major changes in style is that, without proper integration, this sort of thing comes off sounding contrived.

The brass copy-backs *(come sopra)* in **F4-5** (same as **B4-5**) shock us back to jazz reality. The reeds answer in soothing voicings (Am69, E7+5+9) with clarinet lead. Denzal sings the final tonic while Wayne Goodman takes a 2-bar pickup into his trombone solo, with no horn backgrounds. This feels like we are now in small group jazz; a horn solo over the rhythm section.

[Let's listen to everything up to this point, **6-2: A-G**. By the end of the melody chorus, we should feel that the story is complete, but at the same time that we need to explore more.]

Solo Chorus

The Sendoff to the Trombone Solo

On the third beat of **G1**, the brass surprise us by kicking Wayne in the butt. This is a cliché send-off, replete with the customary fall-off. You don't want to do this all the time, but it sure feels right here, since the soloist began his solo with 2½ measures accompanied only by the rhythm section—a preview or teaser. The brass hit on beat 3—implying a 2 feel. I voiced the brass from the second trumpet down on an Am69 in 4ths. The lead trumpet has the 5th on top. His high F# and fall-off are most exciting. For the remainder of this first a section of the tune, there are no horn backgrounds.

Opposite Choir Thumb Line

The saxes (opposite choir from the trombone soloist) play a thumb line the second time around at **G**. The *p* dynamic is essential. So often I hear bands play everything *f* or *ff*—even the backgrounds. This forces the soloist to play *ff*, which is a bit limiting. Notice how the saxes play descending 5ths for the first 4 bars (referencing *motif 2*) and then play an ascending diatonic scale pattern (referencing *motif 1*.)

At **H** the saxes are in simple Drop 2 voicings with an ascending scale-wise melody for four bars, then down a 4th, up a diminished 5th, and finally cadencing down a 3rd on the tonic. These eight measures have the reverse motivic relationship from **G**. As I've said many times in this book and the previous volume, I arrived at this intuitively. Tens of thousands of hours of listening, playing and studying music (jazz and classical) have ingrained these principles deep inside my subconscious.

Backgrounds to the Clarinet Solo

I was thinking about Benny Goodman's band at letter **I**. They often used straight mutes in the brass behind Benny's clarinet solos. Straight mutes decrease the volume of the brass while increasing the brightness. I use 6-part brass voicings here as opposed to the 4- or 5-part voicings that Benny's arrangers normally used. Each of my voicings contains two or three tensions. Note how the brass is voiced in their middle to low registers, so as not to distract from the clarinet. The melody of the lead trumpet uses mostly intervals of 4ths and 5ths (*motif 2*), and the rhythms develop letter **E**. The fall-off in **I6** balances the fall-off in **E1**. It's like when you take off one shoe; you have a strong desire to remove the other one.

One of the nice things about clarinet solos is that you can write both brass and sax backgrounds without confusing the color of the background and foreground.

What starts out as a unison sax/harmonized brass call-and-response evolves into a sax thumb line with a brass interjection (the first three notes from the rhythm of **E3-4**). Some chromatics are injected into the 5ths of the sax thumb line.

Letter **K** is a simple 4-part close *tutti*. I've used 5th intervals throughout. The doubly dotted half/eighth note rhythm of **E1** re-appears in **K1**, **K3**, and **K8**. Again, the middle to low register scoring doesn't compete with the clarinet for attention. Letter **L** gives the clarinet 8 bars with just the rhythm section. This both creates a natural diminuendo and clears our palette for the upcoming return of the vocal.

[Let's listen to the chart so far, **6-3: A-M**. Do the backgrounds feel integral to the piece? Do they develop the motifs sufficiently to keep us interested and curious, without losing the storyline and feeling of the melody?]

Recap

Returning to the Vocal Melody

Although we have just finished a full chorus, I have the vocal come in on the bridge.

Very often we feel that recapping with a full vocal chorus is too long, especially when playing long-form songs like this one.

I want to stay away from the clarinet, since he has just finished his solo. This gives him a chance to sit down and regroup. It also tells the listener that we are in a new section of the chart.

I chose the three bones because starting with 3-part harmony will give us room to grow. I've stayed away from the vocal melody notes to create independence and not confuse the listener as to who is carrying the ball. Since the vocal is moving primarily in quarter notes, which implies a 2 feel, I've written syncopations in a 4 feel for the bones.

For the half-diminished chords, I used the root in conjunction with the flat 5th. This tritone is the defining sound of a half-diminished chord. I omit the 3rd since it doesn't add much color. Notice how I use triads on the C6 and Am7 chords. Just because we know about tensions doesn't mean that we need to use them all the time. Sometimes it's nice to use triads. It adds clarity and (especially in the bones) nobility, which is their natural personality.

The unison pickup to **M3** is so incidental that I didn't want to weigh it down with a voicing. Similarly, the passing diminished on the *and* of 3 in **M3** goes by so quickly that I don't want

to saddle the rhythm section with it. Why disrupt the flow?

Rootless Inversions

The lead trombone melody in **M5-6** moves from one chord tone to another. Since I'm not using low roots, I can simply move each voice down to the next chord tone. I'm not concerned with missing chord tones, since they all get covered in the two inversions. Plus, I like the clarity of the triadic sounds.

To the contrary, I used a 6th in the F#m chord in **M7-8** rather than an F#m triad or F#m7, because I wanted the instability of the tritone between the 6th and minor 3rd of the chord. This instability demands resolution and carries us over the double bar line to letter **N**. Since both the voice and bones are holding out a double whole note, I bring in the octave unison saxes with an ascending 8th note pickup to their upcoming thumb line at **N**. This covers the seam nicely. Rather than just a simple diatonic ascending sax melody, I threw in a few chromatics and a dip in the line.

Brass vs. Reeds

Although letter **N** is essentially brass vs. reeds, I've dressed it up a bit. The sax thumb line references the shape of *motif 2,* but in augmentation and over a different part of the song. *Motif 2* occurs in the second 8 of the a section, but now we are in the second 8 of the bridge. This has a unifying effect.

The brass need to be opposite to the reeds, so that the listener can tell that they are in disagreement. The saxes are in 1; the brass are in 4. The saxes are in octave unison; the brass are in 7-part harmony. The saxes have placid straight rhythms; the brass have agitated syncopations. The saxes play consonant color tones (3rds and 7ths), while the brass play dissonant voicings with lots of tensions.

Brass Rhythms

N1-2 is a development of the figure they played in **E3-4**. This figure is further developed in **N5-6**. The 8th note syncopations give the music forward motion. The trumpets switch gears in **N3-4** and play a unison ascending 8th note scale pattern that develops the sax line from **M7-8**. Again, it's so nice when figures come back. The bones punctuate on the *and* of 2 in both **N3** and **N4**. The fall-off reminds us of the brass fall-off in **G1** and also sets up the brass figure in **N5** nicely. I omitted the 3rd in the C#m7 bone voicing, since the trumpets have the 3rd. Similarly, I omitted the diminished 7th (A) in the C°, since the trumpets play G# to A at that point.

7-part Brass Voicings

On the D#m7-5 I voiced the brass in 3rds, starting with the second trombone, and gave the third bone the 11th on the bottom. I like the minor 9th interval that is created between the third bone and the fourth trumpet—nice and crunchy. I move everyone as little as possible to the next chord. Either they keep a common tone or descend by half step. This lets us focus on the rhythm, rather than on moving pitches.

When a similar figure happens in **N5-6**, I kept everyone as close to his pitches in **N1-2** as possible. I wanted the listener to understand the similarity of **N1-2** and **N5-6**. However, I voiced the Bm7-5 in a completely different way. In **N1-2** the 1st Trumpet has a tension that is doubled two octaves below in the 3rd Trombone. In **N5-6** the 1st Trumpet is on the 7th of the Bm7-5 and is doubled an octave below in the 1st Trombone. The 3rd Trombone has the root, and the 3rd of the chord is in the

3rd Trumpet—a half step above the 9th in the 4th Trumpet and a whole step below the 11th in the 2nd Trumpet. This creates a cluster in the trumpets. No minor 9th intervals in this voicing, but there is a major 7th interval between the -5 and the 11th.

Agreeing with the Singer

The bones join the vocal for six beats in **N7-8**. This texture happened in the same place in the first chorus. This time, I treat the vocal like it is the lead trombone, and voice the three bones below in Drop 2. Then, I shift gears back into 4 for the last two beats adding two syncopations. The E7 gets a +9 in the first bone and a +5 in the vocal. The bones resolve to an anticipated Am6 on the *and* of 4. I've omitted the root since the vocal and bass have it, and the sax/bone unison will be hammering away on four successive A's in **O1-2**.

The Home Stretch

Letter **O** is the last a section. I can feel the end is nigh. It's time to step up the intensity. The saxes and bones are in unison, playing figures that combine the brass figure in **E3-4**, the 5th intervals of *motif 2*, and the chromatics of *motif 3*. The four trumpets with the clarinet on top answer with train whistles. In the **E7-9** the trumpets are voiced as an E7+9 in close position, and the clarinet has the +5 up high, which is a minor 9th above the 5th (B) in the third trumpet. On the F#m7-5, I gave the clarinet a high C but voiced the trumpets as an A#°. This resolves in the next measure to a B7-9.

The trumpets are voiced in close position with the clarinet on the +11 (a major 7th above the third trumpet.) These voicings have a wild effect, with the clarinet in his upper register screaming above the trumpets. By keeping an interval of a 4th above the 1st Trumpet, the clarinet is easily audible in his powerful high register.

Concerted Sax/Bone Voicings

P1-6 keeps the four saxes and three bones together, but now they are in 4-part close harmony with the bones doubling the bottom three saxes. While the vocal sings descending 5ths (*motif 2*), the saxes and bones play ascending scales combining the diatonics of *motif 1* and the chromatics of *motif 3* first in whole notes (with the voice in half notes) and then in half notes when the voice switches to quarter notes.

Tag Ending

Disguising the Symmetry

In most jazz and standard songs, we are dealing with 8 bar phrases. In **No Sign Of You** there are eight 8-bar phrases. Letter **Q** is a tag and letter **R** is the coda. Letter **Q** is 10 bars long, but I start the sax/bone unison line two bars early, so that it overlaps the form, somewhat obscuring the 8-bar blocks. This return to the sax/bone unison feels familiar because of the orchestration, but instead of the rhythmic figures in 4, we're now in 2, first with three syncopations and then, starting at **Q**, implying superimposed meters of 3+3+2+3+5.

The quarter notes are moving predominantly in whole steps (D, E, F#, D, E, F#, C, D, E, D) and ending with a 4-note segment of the diminished scale (D#, E, F#, G). This passage is related to *motif 1*—it's the first three notes, but in D major and then C major, instead of A minor. While this is going on, the vocal has *motif 2* for two bars and *motif 1* for two bars.

While Denzal sings *motif 3* for two bars (**Q5-6**), the clarinet and trumpets return for a measure with the doubly dotted half and 8th rhythm from **E1**. The unstable Bm9-5 has a half step between the 9th and the 3rd, as well as a tritone between the top two voices. This resolves in contrary motion to a Bb13-5 returning to the 4th between the clarinet and first trumpet.

In **Q7-8** the vocal sings the inversion of the sax/bone unison at **Q**, first in quarters, and then stretching out to half notes before changing directions and ascending. While this is going on, the saxes and bones return to 4-part harmony for a measure, but this time they are in Drop 2 with the bari downstairs and the bones doubling the top three saxes. When the vocal is on quarter notes, the saxes and bones are in half notes. When the vocal slows down to half notes, the saxes and bones go back to unison quarter notes with a 4+3+3+2 pattern going from F#° to Dm. The clarinet and trumpets scream a Bm11-5, and then slur down to a *subito mf* in a lower inversion.

Coda

Letter **R** is an 8-bar coda. Denzal sings an ascending 5th slowed down to double whole notes. This is the inversion of *motif 2* in augmentation. Denzal then holds onto the tonic for three bars, releasing just before the drums set up the final chord. During all this, the brass and saxes play the brass figure from **E3-4** in slight variation, before playing the syncopation of *motif 1* in double time, superimposing 3/4 over 4/4. On top of all this and Denzal waiting for "a sign of you," Dan's clarinet plays a 6-measure ascending octave *portamento* resembling a police siren. I swear it didn't even occur to me until we played it, that Dan's gliss is the sign Denzal has been waiting for.

The ensemble voicings have the saxes under the brass for maximum power and weight. The trumpets are in 4-part close harmony for four bars and then upper structure triads for the final four. The bones are tight under the trumpets with root, -5, 7, then 3, 7, +9, then 6, 3, 5 and finally 7, 3, 13 (which just happens to be the same voicing they had on the E7+9.) The saxes have the bari in his bottom register doubling the bass notes. The other three saxes play their own voicings, using notes that mostly double the brass.

[Time to listen again to the entire chart: **6-1: Complete Arrangement**. Does it hold your interest? Is it satisfying? What did you like? What didn't you like? What would you do differently? Do the solos sound integrated? This is not easy to do, especially on a studio date like this, where we didn't have time to let the arrangement gestate with the band for a few weeks. Granted that I know my players and they know my music, this chart still requires serious musicianship from every member of the band.]

The Opposite End Of The Bar

7. The Opposite End Of The Bar

[At www.suchsweetthundermusic.com/pages/cjca2-accompanying-files listen to **7-1: Complete Arrangement.**]

When I was growing up in the 1950s and '60s, there were quite a few variety shows on TV. My mom loved Perry Como and Dinah Shore, and since we only had one TV back then, I watched those shows every week. Later on there was Danny Kaye, Frank Sinatra, Nat Cole, Dean Martin, and my favorite, although short-lived show, Sammy Davis, Jr. There were a pile of other similar shows that I rarely or never watched, like Lawrence Welk, Patti Page, Rosemary Clooney, *Your Hit Parade*, and others. Although there were some comedy routines, dancing and specialty acts (jugglers,

Steve Lawrence and Eydie Gormé in the 1950s. Source: Wikimedia Commons.

magicians, etc.), these shows were about the music. And what music! The American Songbook as sung by the stars and their guests.

There was a house big band or orchestra playing new arrangements written by the top jazz and commercial arrangers of the day. 39 weeks a year, there would be a completely new one-hour show, which contained between 30 and 40 minutes of specially arranged music. Mercifully, they had the 13 summer weeks to recoup, have a nervous breakdown, go on a bender, or whatever they needed to do in order to face another 39-week period of insanity.

Each show had a music director (Nelson Riddle, Paul Weston, Les Brown, George Rhodes,

et al) and a staff of two or three arrangers and three or four copyists. On average each arranger had to churn out at least a chart or two per day, five days a week. Needless to say, they learned how to write quickly. I'm pretty fast, and scoring a vocal chart in a day is normal for me. I don't like to write more than that in one day. My brain needs time to rest and start fresh for the next piece. I've had big projects where I had to write one chart a day for a few weeks, in some cases for as long as 6 weeks—but the thought of 39 weeks without time off really scares me. I have no idea how those guys did it.

The quality of the arrangements on those shows was amazingly good, especially considering the time pressures. The arrangers all had experience writing for the big bands during the 1940s and into the '50s. They brought a jazz perspective to the music on those shows. Some were more commercial than others, but compared to the orchestrations for Broadway shows, TV was much jazzier. And the stars and guests were popular singers who mostly came out of the big bands. Besides the hosts listed above, frequent guests might be Louis Armstrong, Ella Fitzgerald, Sarah Vaughan, Dinah Washington, Tony Bennett, Steve Lawrence and Eydie Gormé—good singers singing good arrangements of good songs, accompanied by a good orchestra. What could go wrong? But by the '70s Americans tastes had changed, and variety shows disappeared.

Sometimes the songs in these shows might be dramatized a bit. Some dialog to set them up, a little choreography or maybe a duet where the singers pretended to be the lovers in the song. This is the genre that **The Opposite End Of The Bar** belongs to. Paul and I envisioned a set with a bar, bartender and several patrons. Perhaps by the end of the song, our protagonist approaches the lady in question. It would be great fun to do this on TV or in a revue.

When he and I were writing songs for these recording sessions with Denzal, Paul emailed me a lyric that he had written but never set to music. He wasn't sure if it would be appropriate for this recording. As was often the case with his lyrics, I knew what the song was before I even finished reading the entire lyric. It took about a half hour to jot down the melody and another hour or so to harmonize it and refine it. If I remember correctly, the arrangement took five or six hours to write. We recorded it exactly as written—no changes or alterations were necessary.

Form

Since this song is a waltz, there are twice as many measures as in similar songs in 4/4. Here is the form: Intro, Verse, Chorus *(aaba)*, ½ chorus *(ba)*, Tag. The *a* sections are 16, 18 and 18 bars; *b* is 24 bars long. The final *a* section at the end of the chart has a tag, which extends it to 20 bars. The intro is 8 bars, followed by a through-composed verse (ABCDEF with lengths of 8, 8, 6, 8, 8, and 8 measures respectively).

What is this song about?

The lyric and music are about insecurity and indecision. The man in the song is afraid to approach an attractive woman at a bar. He thinks that if he is too forward, she will reject him. So small steps seem like a plan. The music conveys all this with the appropriate small steps—minor and major seconds that occasionally venture out to larger intervals and then revert to seconds. Although the verse sets up the story, in order to achieve continuity, the verse also is comprised of minor and major seconds.

Here's what Paul has to say about the lyrics:

"**The Opposite End of the Bar** has a long history. In 1987, I visited New York City for the first time. While there, I watched a scene in a bar where an older woman was attempting to pick up a younger man. An idea for a song suggested itself, and the lyric was written on the plane ride back to the west coast.

I was never entirely satisfied with it, although it was considered good enough to make it into Sheila Davis's book: *The Songwriter's Idea Book*, under the title *The Boy At the Bar*, where it was used to illustrate 'The Stationary Setting.'

The original lyric alternated between the singer's thoughts and what she was saying to the bartender. It could have been made to work by a highly skilled performer, but I don't like to make things harder than they need to be, so I continued to rewrite it. Eventually it became **The Opposite End of the Bar**, a much longer and more carefully developed piece, with the point of view changed to that of a man, and the object of his desire now a woman. What it may have lost in originality, it gained in clarity."

The Verse

Just as it should always be clear to the listener where the intro ends and the song begins, the

THE OPPOSITE END OF THE BAR

Words by Paul Mendenhall
Music by David Berger

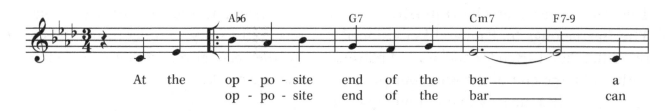

At the op-po-site end of the bar_____ a
op-po-site end of the bar_____ can

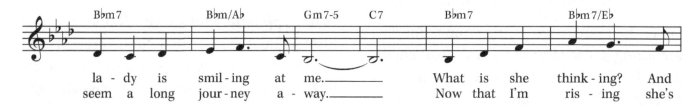

la-dy is smil-ing at me._____ What is she think-ing? And
seem a long jour-ney a-way._____ Now that I'm ris-ing she's

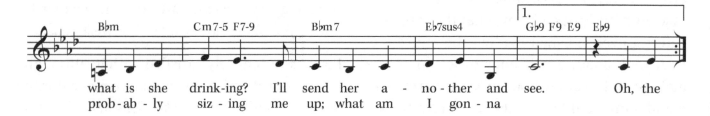

what is she drink-ing? I'll send her a-no-ther and see. Oh, the
prob-ab-ly siz-ing me up; what am I gon-na

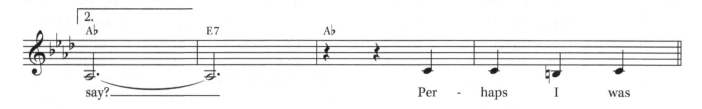

say?_____ Per-haps I was

wrong_____ to make the first move._____ I've put my-self on the

spot._____ And com-ing on strong_____ can be the worst

Example 7-1: Lead sheet © 2010 Such Sweet Thunder

verse and chorus must be clearly delineated. In most cases verses are either sung out of tempo, or accompanied by just one instrument, or both. For this song, the verse is in tempo and uses the full complement of instruments.

Although I changed textures when the chorus came in, it wasn't enough to establish the re-

The Opposite End of the Bar

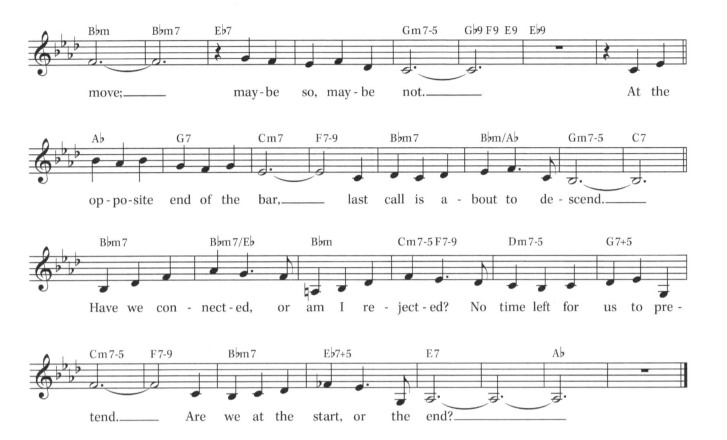

lease we should feel at the chorus. Rather than mess with the orchestration, I asked Denzal to speak the verse. We realized quickly that that was too extreme—it sounded contrived. Plus I missed hearing the melody of the verse. So we wound up having him talk just one phrase of the verse, and that was enough.

Recitativo

Honestly, I don't remember if I composed the verse or the chorus first. I think I started with the verse. Verses come out of the opera tradition. In opera, everything is sung. In between the songs the dialog is sung. This is called *recitativo* or recitative, or sometimes shortened to *recit* (which sounds too informal, to me, for opera). Recitatives can be sung, spoken, or a combination of both. They have (or should have) a conversational tone.

Rather than going directly from speaking dialog to singing a song, we can set up the song with a verse that is more songlike than recitative, but not so much as the chorus.

Nearly every song in a book show is preceded with a verse. The verse is always included in the sheet music, though not in fake books. Most often the verses are not played in instrumental versions, and not even sung by most vocalists, outside of Broadway or cabaret. Frank Sinatra was famous for singing the verses to some songs. Most verses are obscure and have only a peripheral musical relationship to the song. However, some verses are so excellent that I am disappointed when they are *not* performed, e.g. *Stardust*, and many Cole Porter and Gershwin songs.

I love how singing the verse not only establishes theatricality, but gives us time to tell the story and provides material to extend the arrangement beyond 32 bars. Although verses are generally sung before the chorus (as in this arrangement), they can also be sung between choruses, or both (if there are two sets of lyrics to the verse, as in *I Was So Young, You Were So Beautiful*).

Sometimes when I start writing a song, I don't know what key it is in until it comes to a cadence or, in some cases, until I get to the final cadence. Sometimes I don't know what the meter is. Are those three quarter notes or a quarter note triplet? Sometimes I go back and forth with this decision. This was not the case for even a second on **The Opposite End Of The Bar**. I knew from the first sentence that it was a waltz.

It was one of those lyrics where I heard the rhythms and pitches mostly simultaneously when reading the lyric for the first time. Although the verse has a slightly asymmetrical construction, and the song itself doesn't sound like any other song I know, this was one of the easiest songs I have ever written. My first reaction to it was, "How could the music ever be anything but this?" That is always a good sign.

Hit Songs

I once asked Michel Legrand if he ever knew when one of his songs would become a hit. He told me that he never did. I've never written a hit, so unlike Michel, I can't answer that question, but I can tell when a song (or an arrangement) works and when it doesn't. Sometimes a bit of tinkering is called for; sometimes a major overhaul, and sometimes I cut my losses and start all over from scratch.

Basically I'm just trying to write music that, if I were in the audience, I would like to hear.

Collaboration is Tricky

I've worked with a number of lyricists over the years, and each relationship and work process was different from the others. I don't think one was better than another, just different. Some lyricists have told me that they hear the music in their head when writing lyrics and write the lyric to fit the melody and rhythms that they hear. Paul told me that he often did this. When I asked him to sing his music, he usually declined, telling me that it wasn't very good, or that it was someone else's famous song, that it was better for me not to know. He also told me that he was surprised by the music I put to his lyric—that it was nothing like what he had imagined, and that he would need to sing the song through a few times to get used to it. Fair enough.

"Hey, Babe, we're not married to it"

I once worked briefly with a fledgling lyricist who told me that my music was nothing like what he heard when he was writing the words. I asked him why, then, did he need me? Why not just use his music? He said that his music wasn't any good. The problem was that he was stuck on his music and couldn't let it go. Imagination and flexibility are key to success in this business. Mel Brooks said that when Sid Caesar rejected a sketch for *Your Show of Shows,* the writers would respond with, "Hey, Babe, we're not married to it."

Simple vs. Complex

If you look at the harmonic scheme for the verse, it can be reduced to a series of dominant/tonic relationships. I've dressed it up a bit with *ii* chords and few other passing chords

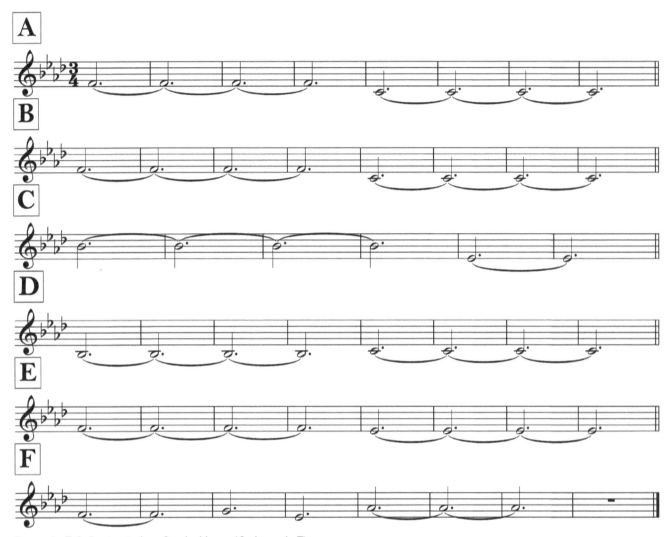

*Example 7-2: Basic pitches for the Verse (**A** through **F**).*

and substitutions, but the idea was to keep it simple and leave the more interesting melodic and harmonic material for the refrain. This simple/complex relationship for the verse and refrain is quite common.

Basic Pitches

Let's reduce the melody of the verse (pick-up to letter **A** through letter **F**) to its basic pitches (*Example 7-2*).

Simple, right? Notice how I avoid landing on the tonic until the end of the verse. Actually, the great majority of verses end on the dominant, and then resolve to the tonic on the downbeat of the refrain. Ending on the tonic is effective here because of what the lyric says

at that point. There is a feeling of finality, like the guy in the song's problem is solved. When he says, "Except for the one who just got my attention." At this point there is a great feeling of hope and enthusiasm. He has come out of his funk. Now we have closed that dark chapter and are starting on a new, exciting and scary romantic adventure.

Auxiliary Melody Notes

In the 46 measures of this almost exclusively diatonic verse, there are exactly four accidentals, and all four are blue notes (three B♮s and a D♮—flat 3rds leading up to a flat 5th). Each is used as a chromatic lower neighbor just to add a tiny bit of spice. Three of the accidentals fall on the downbeat of the fifth measure of their 8-bar phrase (an *appoggiatura* resolving to the tonic chord). In order to accommodate these blue notes, I use either a tonic diminished chord (Ab°) or a bVI7 (E7). These two chords are used as passing and *appoggiatura* chords throughout the entire arrangement in the accompaniment, thus contributing to the gentle chromaticism of the piece.

The character in the song becomes the character *of* the song.

When I first read the lyric, it seemed to be naturally smooth, hence the predominance of scale-wise movement. The few larger intervals are well placed with the natural stresses and inflections of the words and give the verse the appropriate character. No jerky motions here. The guy in the song is shy. He proceeds with caution and doesn't want to draw attention to himself.

Although the character of the song must have continuity from the verse to the refrain, it is crucial for the drama and the listeners' interest that the opposites be out in force in terms of rhythm, melody, harmony and orchestration.

Rhythm: The rhythm of the melody is reversed, from phrases starting with a long note followed by quarter notes, to phrases starting with quarter notes followed by a long note.

Melody: The quarter notes form descending and ascending diatonic scales. When you eliminate the ornamental pitches (upper and lower neighbors, *appoggiaturas* etc.), the basic pitches change every bar or two for the *a* section (**G** and **H**) and revert to 4-bar stretches for the bridge (**I** and **J**) much like the verse.

Harmony: The verse starts on the *ii* chord. The refrain starts on the tonic.

Orchestration: The trombone thumb line creates stability and continuity that are lacking in the verse.

Here are the basic pitches (minus ornamentation) for the refrain (**G** through **L**, *Example 7-3*). The remainder of the chart repeats previous sections until the optimistic turn in the penultimate measure.

This basic foundation for the melody was not planned consciously. I was just composing one note per syllable of the lyric, and left the structure to my intuition. Where the melody ascended, descended, and changed course had as much to do with the natural inflection of the words as it did with making an attractive melody. Satisfying both criteria is essential in creating a good song.

Adding Harmony

I began by creating a bass line to accompany the melody, and didn't assign chord names until after the entire bass line was completed. The melody/bass relationship sounds complete. Adding other chord notes merely adds color. I've used mostly diatonic chords, some of which are preceded by their secondary dominants. In some cases I used inversions to fill in passing tones in the bass line (**G6**). The minor 9ths on the dominants sweeten the mood, as does the diminished 5th on the Cm7-5 in **H4**. The Gb is a blue note in Ab, which is very welcome and sets up the turnaround in **H7** as well as the important surprise *bVII* chord on the provocative word, "strong" in **J5**. It doesn't hurt that the melody is the +11.

*Example 7-3: Basic pitches for the refrain (**G** through **L**).*

An Even Bigger Harmonic Surprise

The Ab° passing and *appoggiatura* chords of the verse are pushed one step further in the refrain to become surprise E7 chords (♭VI). This compelling sound is introduced in the phrase extension in **H10** and then brought back for the penultimate measure of the chart. I've loved the ♭VI (also known as the shoulder chord) ever since I first heard *Mood Indigo* as a child. The combination of the unusual bass note, the two blue notes (♭3 and ♭5) and the tempering enharmonic use of the tonic as the 3rd of the chord is so sensual.

[I suggest that you listen to the entire track while reading the lead sheet. Disregard the arrangement. Just focus on Denzal's melody, the bass and the harmony, and how they help the words to tell the story. If I've done my job correctly, this song could be performed effectively in a cabaret setting with just voice and piano.]

The Intro

The intro should tell the whole story, except that if we've never heard this chart, we won't exactly know what it means yet. This song is about a man overcoming his shyness and fear of rejection, and acting the part of an alpha male approaching an attractive woman at a bar. In this instrumental introduction I give Bob Millikan (lead trumpet—our most alpha male!) the solo role. He plays in opposition to the rest of the brass section. They are stuck repeating *ii7-5 V7-9* of B♭m and finally move on to C7 B7, which still doesn't get us to our A♭ tonic resolution. Are we feeling frustrated? I hope so, because our hero is frustrated with his own ambivalence. The D♮s in the trumpet (13ths on the F7-9s) are his bold attempts at moving forward, but he keeps getting pulled back.

5-Part Close Brass Voicings

The brass is voiced in 5-part close voicings below the solo trumpet. This gets a tight sound. It doesn't have much weight. I'll save the weight for when I put the roots on the bottom in **mm7-8**. Opening up the voicings like this gives a cadential feeling—in this case, B7, a tritone substitute of F7, a semi-cadence in B♭m.

Unison Doubling Within a Voicing

I generally do not double at the unison within a section in voicings, but in **measure 7**, Trumpets 2 and 3 are doubled for one note. I didn't hear another pitch in that voicing. I didn't want to disturb the tritone relationship between the solo trumpet and the other trumpets. Since everyone's line feels good, I'm going to go with the doubling. There's no logic in having one of the trumpets rest for that measure—that would be awkward.

Why Only Three Trumpets?

Since I have four trumpets in my band, why is this chart written for three? I grew up listening to Fletcher Henderson, Basie before 1939, Ellington and Lunceford before 1942, Gerry Mulligan and a pile of other bands that used three trumpets. Playing in a section like that is a lot of fun. There is an intimacy you just don't get with four. As Bob Brookmeyer used to say, once you have four, you are dealing with an institution; you need to buy uniforms...

I like having four trumpets in my band for two purposes: 4-part trumpet *solis* and supporting high first trumpet parts. Since I'm not a big fan of doubling brass notes (even at the octave), and most voicings don't involve more than 5 or 6 notes, a lot of the time I am writing for fewer than 7 brass players. The flavor of this particular chart is quaint and sweet—definitely not powerful. I didn't envision any trumpet solis, so I opted to let Brandon Lee sit this one out, since he had a bunch of solos on the other charts in this recording session.

Although some bandleaders would never entertain anything less than a full complement playing every chart, Ellington and Strayhorn both wrote many charts for three trumpets even while there were four or five in the band.

Symphony orchestras don't feel compelled to have everyone play every piece. I'm not saying that I do this a lot, but I'm going to reserve the right to have tacet sheets where applicable.

The Verse

As I've said before, it's important to establish that the intro is over and that we are in the meat of the chart. A severe change of orchestration is one of the most obvious means of accomplishing this. Since we haven't heard from the reeds in the intro, they are an obvious choice at **A** for the verse.

Vocal/Reed Counterpoint

I'm looking for a smooth and somewhat secure feeling, so I've assigned sustained roots of the chords to the bass clarinet and sustained pads in the tenor and clarinet. The two flutes answer the vocal voiced in 3rds before joining the lower voices in pads when the vocal moves to 8th notes. It's simple counterpoint—when the vocal rests or holds out a note, the reeds are active, and when the vocal is active, the reeds sustain or rest.

Furthermore, I'm careful to stay away from the vocal pitches in the top reed part. Although much opera and Broadway orchestration doubles the vocal line in the accompanying instruments, I rarely do that. The more independent the voice is, the more we understand his role as representing *us*—the individual vs. the rest of the world. Also, in jazz, we like the voice to be free to interpret his part, without conflicting with an instrument that is in unison with him. And as I've also said previously, when the voice is doubled in an instrument, the words are obscured. Since the words are primary for understanding the story, we need to help the listener hear them as much as possible.

5-Part Reed Voicings

Since there are five reeds, I am afforded the luxury of using five different pitches per voicing. For the most part, this is the case, but when it becomes inconvenient, I relax into 4-part voicings. This alternation between 5- and 4-part writing is established immediately in the first two measures at **A**. In **A1** both flutes play A♭s, which are doubled an octave below in the tenor. In **A2** the lower reeds again provide root, 3rd and 7th; but now the flutes start and end the measure with upper structure 9ths, 11ths, and 13ths. The passing tone in the middle of the bar has the flutes on the 3rd and 5th; the 3rd doubles the tenor at the octave, creating a 4-part voicing. **A3** and **A4** are both 5-part voicings.

Since the voice is pretty much sustained in **A5-7** over a basically A♭ tonic chord, I kept the bass clarinet on a sustained A♭ and had the other four reeds alternate between A♭° and A♭ major chords (with either added 6ths or major 7ths). The scale-wise quarter note movement answers the vocal line in **A3-4** both in speed and shape. The return to 5-part in **A8** is celebrated with a tension of the passing A° in the top flute. I was very careful to make sure that each reed part has a strong melody for all of letter **A**.

Low-Register Reed Scoring

Although the bottom octave of the flute lacks the power and volume of the upper octaves, I particularly like its gentle and vulnerable sound. I'm not alone in this respect. Gil Evans' use of low-register C flute as well as alto flute and bass flute inspired other jazz arrangers to use these sounds. For the most part, this has been reserved for the recording studio, where close miking can overcome the natural imbalance with the rhythm section.

Once the drummer hits the cymbal or closes the hi-hat, we lose the flutes. With this in mind, I've instructed Jimmy Madison to omit the hi-hat and softly play brushes on the snare. I learned this little trick 50 years ago from Ray Wright, and it still works. Ray did this for accompanying strings, but the same principle applies to woodwinds. Of course, the bass and piano must not be amplified.

Word Painting

Denzal says, "noisy" at **B**, so I have the brass (who were *tacet* for **A**, and will sound fresh) answer with a rhythmic figure in straight mutes, which sound a bit like a noisy ratchet. Note how they move in 3rds, similar to the flutes at **A**, but just down and up, as opposed to the flutes' down, up, down, up. The short quarters in the brass give it the rhythmic quality and also draw our attention to this rude interruption to the smooth setting. I've got six brass at my disposal, so I'm going to take advantage of that and use 6-part voicings (5-part over a root in the bottom trombone). The passing B7 is the tritone sub of F7 (the dominant of the upcoming B♭m7).

Conversely, when Denzal says, "quiet" in **B5**, the reeds answer with a legato, slurred 8th note passage that combines the step-wise quarter notes and alternating 3rds of **A**. For added fun, I had the reeds alternate between A♭maj7 and A♭°, thereby reversing the relationships established in **A**—diatonic 3rds in 8th notes and scale-wise passing tonic diminished chords in quarter notes become alternating 3rds in 8th notes that also alternate between A♭maj9 and A♭°.

Pinkies Up

My first year in college, I played in the freshman concert band under a very colorful conductor named Ed Gobrecht. He constantly talked about making music, as opposed to playing notes. He would encourage us to play a passage as if we were "goosing butterflies." He would have us close our eyes and feel the energy rising from the floor and coursing through our legs, torso and heads. In describing one polite passage, he told us to imagine that we were sipping tea, and then admonished us for not lifting our pinkies. This verse has that same attitude of gentility—hence the pseudo-triangle note in the drums in **B7**. I love metaphors and dead metaphors. Which reminds me of a great Phil Seamen story.

Stop me if you've heard this one.

My buddy Joe Temperley loved to talk about his London days working with eccentric musicians like Tony Coe and Phil Seamen. Phil, in addition to being the best drummer in England during the 1950s and '60s, was a terrible junkie. Leonard Bernstein loved him and hired him for a run of *West Side Story*. One night Phil nodded off during the performance and woke up in a panic. Thinking that he had missed his gong entrance, he gave the gong a good whack. Unfortunately this was a very quiet and intimate spot in the show. Everyone onstage and in the audience gasped, and the show came to an immediate standstill. Phil realized what had happened. He stood up in his tuxedo, puffed out his chest, and announced, in his best imitation of a snooty English butler, "Dinner is served."

Developing Ideas

The key is to reuse material, re-combine it in different ways and gradually develop it by building on the changes we've made as we go along. We want to avoid introducing new material. Everything must relate to previous material. In fact this entire chart was set up in the seemingly innocuous introduction.

Look at the solo trumpet line: ascending minor 2nd, ascending perfect 5th, ascending major 2nd, repeat 2nds, repeat 2nds, down major 6th, up major 2nd, up minor 6th, down major 2nd, down minor 3rd. If we invert the 6ths to 3rds, they become major and minor 3rds, leaving us with 2nds, 3rds and a lone ascending perfect 5th. I don't recall if I wrote the intro first or later on, but I do know that I wasn't consciously thinking about any of this stuff. The trumpet line just popped into my head, and I ran with it. Of course it didn't hurt that I've heard thousands of waltzes like this during my lifetime, especially while I was growing up and this sort of music was popular).

Letter **C** develops the ideas set forth in **B**. The rhythmic brass (I've added two pick-up notes and used octave jumps to increase the rhythmically disjointed character) are answered by the legato reeds which move in 2nds and 3rds with smooth passing chords, but this time they have expanded into their upper register.

Elision

The phrase at **C** is elided. We have come to expect 8-bar phrases, but this section gets squeezed together, so that there are only six bars before we land solidly on the word, "patter" at letter **D**. I love when asymmetrical phrases feel completely normal. I read something to the same effect in liner notes on a Horace Silver record once. Composers love to do daring things, but the key is to not sound weird (unless you are really trying to be weird). Music is not a science project. We are telling a story. Especially when lyrics are involved.

More Development

Letter **D** continues to develop the material of letter **C**. The brass adds more octaves to its answer and then follows with a sustained Eb13+11 chord. The reeds play an ascending scale with passing diminished chords. They start with quarter notes and switch to 8ths. Again the voicings are 4-part close with the bass clarinet holding out a tonic below the other reeds. This leads to a 2-bar break as in letter **B**, except that this time, there is a drum fill for one bar and a sustained reed F7+9 chord, mimicking the brass chord from four bars earlier.

Time for a Change

Letter **E** starts with "prospects." Not only do I feel that we need a change in texture and orchestration, but "prospects" has a positive connotation to it. **E1-3** has a chromatically ascending dotted half note thumb line in the unison bottom three reeds that morphs into our old friend, the upward diatonic scale in quarter notes.

Re-harmonizing with Upper Structure Triads

In **E4-5** we expect Eb7 to Ab, since that is what happened in that spot in **A**, **B**, and **D**. The tip-off to me that something different was needed is the Ab on beat 2 of the melody in **A4**. That would at least necessitate an Eb7sus4—but why not think a little more outside the box and start to be more courageous?

My first thought was to use Db7 for the bar and then resolve to Ab. The D♮ downbeat of **E5** suggested a tonic diminished (Ab°) resolving on beat 2 to Ab. We've heard a lot of that, so it's a possibility. Or the D♮ could be the 7th of an E7 (shoulder chord). Ooh! Nice! Now we can work backwards to its dominant B7 (F is the +11 melody), and chromatically upwards C7 (A♭ is the +5 melody), and D♭7 (B♭ is the 13th melody). So I got the D♭7 that I started with, but was able to re-harmonize all the melody notes.

For the three chords in **E4** I gave the tenor and bass clarinet the 3rd and 7th of each chord. The clarinet has the melody an octave above the vocal (it's on the inside of 5-part voicings, so it will go unnoticed by listeners, but help to make the vocal feel comfortable). The two flutes and clarinet are voiced in upper structure triads (E♭/D♭7, A♭/C7, D♭/B7.) The E7 downbeat of **E5** resolves to a root position E7+9 in a stable 1,5,3,7,+9 voicing—an unstable, unresolved chord in a stable voicing with root, 5th on the bottom.

Although **E6** is a G7-9+5 voiced in 4-part close in the bottom four reeds, the top flute outlines an upper structure E♭ triad just to tease us. His top E♭ leads to an F on the downbeat of E7, the 11th of the Cm7.

Big Jumps

We are all taught that good voice leading means stepwise or common tone movement in the inside parts, but sometimes it's effective to have all the voices leap in the same direction. This happened on the E7+9 in **E5** (downward jump), so, I'm going to balance that with an upward jump to the Cm11 in **E7**. Notice that I avoided the 9th (D♮) since it is not in the key (A♭) and there is a D♭ in the next measure.

I'm going to jump down once again to the F7-9 in **E8** and also recall the stand-alone dotted half notes in **D4** and **D8**. The voicing is Drop 2 over a low root in the bass clarinet.

Wrappin' It Up

Our verse is coming to a close and I feel the need to do something more spectacular to top what's gone on before, and make a brilliant finish to set up the refrain.

Re-harmonization

For starters let's re-harmonize the melody. I'm going to keep the starting *ii* chord and tonic resolution in their usual places (**F1** and **F5**), but we can use dominant and chromatic motion to get to the tonic, and then embellish the tonic with our old friend the tonic diminished (A♭°) and a surprise ♭*II* chord (Amaj9+11).

When I harmonize and re-harmonize, I always start with the melody and then create a bass line that has a strong melody and makes a good tension/release relationship with the melody. In order to get to the A♭ in **F5**, I approach it from a half step above. This works well, since the melody is a tritone away from the bass. I can use an A7-5. I'll precede that with its dominant (E7). The G melody makes a +9. I like the sensual sound of that in this spot. I'll precede the E7 with its dominant (B7). The D♭, E♭, F melody works nicely on the B7 (9th, 3rd, ♭5th). I'm not concerned with the relationship from the B♭m7 to the B9. The B9 can (and should be) a surprise, or at least a fresh sound.

Putting It All Together

At letter **F** I'm going to bring back as many of the orchestrational ideas as I can, and reorganize them in such a way as to create tension, which will be resolved on the downbeat of **G**.

1. I'm going to take the singular sustained chord that we just heard in **E8** and recreate it using a D♭ upper structure triad on the B9 in **F2**.

2. The bottom four reeds play pads for two bars while the top flute plays the rhythm and shape of **A1**; only this time, he plays it two bars later in the phrase (**F3**) and repeats it (**F4**). The intervals are expanded from the original 3rds to perfect 4ths and then augmented 4ths. Due to the unexpected substitute chords and the interesting melodic motion of the flute melody, I'm not concerned that the flute notes double the vocal and second flute in **F3** and the bass and vocal in **F4**. *If it sounds good, it is good.*

3. The top four reeds go back to their ascending scale voiced in 4-part close using an appoggiatura tonic diminished over the sustained tonic in the bass clarinet in **F5**.

4. The brass play a stand-alone sustained chord in **D4**, but when it is referenced in **F6**, they finish it off with a button on the break in **F7**. The repeated dominant note (Eb) in the lead trumpet is reminiscent of the repeated notes in the "noisy" effect of the verse. The six brass are voiced with upper structure triads (Abm/A, Eb/Ab6). Having the brass play open increases their volume and intensity.

5. The three bottom reeds echo the brass long/short, but start on beat 2 in **F7**, creating a syncopation. They repeat the tonic diminished/major motif that we've been playing with all along (Ab°, Abmaj9). The flutes arpeggiate up the Ab° triad with our minor 3rd motif, before resolving to the Ab chord, which is voiced in 5ths (Ab, Eb, Bb, F, C).

So much of jazz is based on tertian harmony. It's refreshing to build chords in major 2nds, perfect 4ths, perfect 5ths or minor 7ths. These neutral intervals have a completely different feel. Of course 4th voicings were so overused in the 1960s and '70s that they became a cliché. Reserved for the right spot, they can still be surprising and effective.

Now we are ready for the action to begin.

[Let's listen to the intro and the verse (7-2: **A-G**). Have I piqued your interest? Do you want to hear what happens to our hero? In songs like this, the music helps to tell the story in the lyrics. As much as I'm trying to make the music sound interesting, I have to be careful not to distract from the plot and character development in the words. On the other hand, I want the music to be interesting enough to add color to the character and his story, and pique the listener's curiosity about how it will turn out.]

The Refrain

Do you remember the ascending perfect 5th leap in the pick-up to the intro? Finally, here is the payoff. We have the reeds voiced in 5ths followed by a pick-up into the refrain at **G**, again leaping up a 5th.

"At the opposite…"

The word "opposite" in the lyric tells us what we need at **G**—as different an orchestration as possible from what came before. The rhythm section remains the same as before, so it is up to the horns to make everything feel fresh. I can change the texture and the orchestration. Instead of chordal backgrounds, we can have a unison line.

We haven't heard anything from the trombones as a section. They've only played a supporting role under the trumpets. How about if they play a unison counter-line to the vocal? The idea is to have the bones play long notes while the voice sings quarter notes, and vice versa. Also, I will avoid the vocal and bass pitches in the bones. At the same time I need to give the bones a good melody that they will enjoy playing and will sound good on its own. This is good for 14 bars.

The Turnaround

My first thought was to make the C in the vocal part in **H7** the +11 of a G♭7 chord and descend chromatically to the dominant (E♭7). So I could voice two trumpets and three bones in 13+11 chords built up in 3rds. Remember the solo trumpet in the intro? Finally, he comes back with a retrograde of the last three notes he played in the intro. In the intro he has E♭, D♭, B♭. Backwards would be B♭, D♭, E♭. Let's repeat the first note at the end: B♭, D♭, E♭, B♭, and transpose it up a 4th: E♭, G♭, A♭, E♭. Until now, I always wondered why I wrote this trumpet line, but now I see why it sounds good to me.

Adding an Element the Second Time Around

One of the most basic concepts in arranging is to start simply and add an element on the repeat of a section. I'm not ready for the trumpets yet; I want to hold them off until the bridge, so that section will feel opposite to the preceding two *a* sections. That leaves me with the reeds. In **G1** I have them play a syncopated answer to the bones, giving the reeds the rhythm of **bar 2** of the intro and adding a trill for motion. Trills are idiomatic and easy to play on reed instruments.

This figure repeats whenever the bones play a sustained note. I only use four reeds (omitting the Tenor) because 4-part harmony is enough. All the voicings are in Drop 2 spacing. Notice how I avoided the trombone pitches. The only vocal pitch that is doubled in the top flute is in **G2**. I did this to make it clear to the listener that I am repeating the figure from **G1**. Once

this is established, I can move the melody more freely.

Reversing Roles for the Cadence

In the second ending, the bones continue in unison for two notes before switching roles with the reeds (the bones provide a chord for the octave unison reeds.) We've been using tonic diminished chords for the cadences in the verse. It might be nice to give the reeds the line they had over the tonic diminished in F7, but resolve down to the dominant instead of chromatically up to the 3rd of the tonic. The bones play A♭° to A♭ major triad, but the bass plays an E below the A♭°, making an E7 (shoulder chord). We had a brief shoulder chord earlier on in **E5**, but holding it for three beats makes it more prominent here and adds to the character of the piece.

Breaks

Notice how often phrases end with breaks. This is a big part of the character of this arrangement. After all, the lyric is about ambivalence. Our hero starts to make a move and then stops when he gets scared.

Finding "New" Opposites for the Bridge

This song has a 24-measure bridge, which is a bit odd. 16 bars would be normal, but in this case, 24 bars feels right. Since letters **G** and **H** have been dealing with unison bones and harmonized reeds, a recognizable opposite would be harmonized brass (trumpets over bones) and unison reeds.

6-part Brass Voicings Using Upper Structure Triads

Do you remember the syncopated brass figure in **measure 1** of the intro? If you were wondering when that would come back, here it is at last. I expect that your conscious mind had forgotten about it. But if Sigmund Freud taught us anything, it's that the unconscious holds onto things that the conscious mind has let go. As in the intro, I keep the top trumpet note the same when the chord changes on the second bar. But unlike the intro, I repeat the rhythm of the first bar, rather than altering it.

While Denzal is holding out "wrong," the brass provide the forward motion. Since he is still holding out his note in **I3**, I added a button. The voice leading is very smooth—either common tones or half steps. The upper structure voicings are Ab/Bbm, Cm/Eb7-9, and back to Ab/Bbm. I use the same rhythmic figure four bars later over different chord changes: Eb/Fm, G/F7. In this case all the voices jump up a 3rd to grab our attention.

Let's agree to disagree.

Okay, I know I said that I try to avoid using the same pitches in the foreground and background—so how come the lead trumpet and the vocal have Eb unisons in **I1-3** and Bb unisons in **I5-6**? Good question. The reason for avoiding unisons (for the most part) is that too much agreement makes for no drama. But sometimes it's interesting to have two exposed parts agree while inside parts are in disagreement. This is what is happening here.

The lead trumpet is giving us the agreement that we expected in the resolution of the a section of the song (**H9**). Denzal resolves his line to the tonic (Ab), but the horns won't give him that satisfaction. The 2nd Trombone does have a couple of Ab's, but they are hidden inside the voicings. When the lead trumpet finally agrees with the vocal, it serves to make the

dissonant brass voicings sound quite normal and pleasant.

Beware of Greeks Bearing Gifts

In letter **I**, I've set up an easily digestible foreground/background relationship between the vocal and the brass. Look what happens at **J**. The brass repeats what they played in **I1-3**, but the vocal now sings a Bb. Instead of being in unison with the lead trumpet, he is with the 3rd Trombone and the bass. Four bars later, the brass repeat the rhythmic figure, but this time the lead trumpet Ebs are the 13th of a Gb13+11 chord with the vocal on the +11 (C). The voicing is Ab/Gb7, resolving to an F7+5 voiced as Db/F7-9.

Note the unusual use of the flat 9th in the bottom trombone. Since the lead trumpet is on the F root, the 3rd Trombone's Gb (the flat 9th) makes the voicing unstable. I like that instability, which makes it necessary to have eight more measures of bridge before we get back to the *a* section of the song.

What To Do with the Reeds

The brass and vocal are pretty much complete at **I** and **J**, but as long as I've got five reeds, this is a good opportunity to have them interact with the brass and build to a climax on the button at **J7**.

Call-and-Response

The reeds answer the brass figures in letter **I**. The first three notes are unison upward chromatics in the bottom three reeds, followed by a syncopated 5-note chord (Ab/C7 upper structure triad). This is the syncopation that we heard in the bottom three reeds in **F7**. It's nice when things come back.

The re-harmonization in **I7-8** is quite sophisticated with its interesting vocal melody/bass line relationship and its variety of chord qualities. Some of the chords are diatonic and some are chromatic. Now look at the interesting relationship between the vocal and the top flute. Essentially they are in contrary motion. Also, they mostly use the same intervals, but inverted. The voice has minor 2nd, minor 3rd, major 3rd, minor 3rd, minor 2nd. The flute has minor 2nd, minor 3rd, major 2nd, minor 2nd.

Sectional Integrity

The reeds are mostly voiced in upper structure triads and are designed to sound good by themselves. I strive to write good melodies for everyone, and to have each part sound good in combination with all the other parts. On top of that, I like to have each section feel complete within itself. This makes for better performances, less rehearsal time, and happier section players.

Pulling Out All the Stops

If letters **I** and **J** correspond to the shout chorus in an instrumental chart, then letter **I** is the set-up and **J** is the payoff. Whereas the brass and reeds neatly and politely stay away from each other and obey the call-and-response convention in **I**, in **J** the two sections relate in more complex contrapuntal ways. The reeds begin **J** with an ascending diatonic line that becomes chromatic. Rather than have the 7th of the B♭m7 resolve in the normal downwards direction to the 3rd of E♭7, I have the A♭ continue up chromatically to the +11 of E♭7.

This is somewhat surprising, especially since the A♮ is not in the brass voicing, and the vocal is a half step away on a Bb. Denzal is a big boy. He can handle the rub. This scale-wise ascending line with three quarter notes and a dotted half is similar to much of the reed material on the verse. In **J3-4** the reeds play unison ascending 3rds and land on an E♭13+11 (upper structure triad F/E♭7). I rarely use so many upper structure triads, but they seem to be in character for this piece.

Reversing Roles with the Brass

Remember the good old days of letter **I**, where the lead trumpet was in unison with the vocal and bass in **I2**? Since the lead trumpet in **J5-7** is not doubling the vocal or bass, I'm going to give the reeds a fast 8th note line that alternates between the bass note (G♭ root) and the vocal note (C, which is the +11). I'm looking for excitement from the agitated movement in the reeds. Their tritone intervals (G♭'s and C's) are interesting enough and help to ground us harmonically.

I like how this unstable tritone interval (it divides the octave in half) contributes to the stability of this phrase.

Then, just when we think we are safe, the reeds end on a B♮ button. This is the +11 of the F7 chord and is not in the 6-note brass voicing. It creates an unstable relationship with the root in the lead trumpet and bass.

Calming Things Down

The ascending unison chromatic line in the reeds reappears in the trombones in **K1-4**. This time it is completely chromatic (all dotted half notes), and instead of ending on the volatile A♮ (+11 of the E♭7), it ascends to the stable 5th of the E♭9, thereby completing the line that was unfinished eight measures before. Not so fast. The reeds answer the bones in **K5** with a Gm7-5. They use the syncopated rhythmic figure that the brass played in the first bar of the intro. The interesting thing here is the first flute's return to A♮ (the 9th of Gm7-5). The trumpets and bones then answer the reeds with their turnaround from **H7-8**. Whoa! Wait a minute! This figure comes a bar early in the phrase.

I love when the symmetry is disrupted and it still feels right.

Clearing the Palate

Letters **L** through **M** *tacet* all the horns and give the accompaniment over to the rhythm section. Until now Isaac ben Ayala has just been playing oom pah pah. The point of having a creative pianist in your band is moments like this, when he adds his unique point of view to the story. We've been hearing wall-to-wall horns for the whole chart until now. We've got 18 bars before we *D.S.* back to the bridge and let the horns carry us for the rest of the piece. When the brass enters, we will fully appreciate them, since we haven't heard any horns in so long.

The Coda

Actually, what is marked as the coda is labeled as such purely for practical purposes (saving paper). What we have is the recapitulation of the first 12 bars of the *a* section of the refrain—this time without the reeds. I'm omitting the reeds in order to wind down towards the ending.

At the beginning of a chart, we generally add elements. To prepare for the end, we often subtract.

Tag Ending

What we have at **N5** is not really a coda, but a tag ending. At **N** we expect *ii V ii V I* in the first five bars, since that has happened before.

In order to give the piece finality, four bars have been added. Paul built this into the chart with his lyric. I just had to adjust the melody and chord changes to make this tag sound natural.

The first thing I knew was that the final *ii V* would occur in **N9-12**, so I needed to get to that ii smoothly—hence the Cm7-5 F7-9 (*ii7-5 V* of B♭m). Instead of cadencing in **N5** with the normal A♭ chord, I used a deceptive cadence: *I ii7-5 V* into Cm in **N5-6** (Dm7-5 G7+5). This is especially nice, since the D root of the Dm7-5 is a tritone away from the expected A♭. The Dm7-5 is preceded by Cm7-5 F7-9 in **N4**. We expect to resolve that F7-9 to a B♭m7, but instead, the bass walks down the scale (F, E♭, D).

Tying Up All the Loose Ends

From **N5** to the end of the chart, I need to tie up any loose ends and make a strong motivic statement. Let's see how many of our motifs appear:

1. In **N5-6** the reeds play a syncopated sustained note much as they did in **G** the second time (minus the trill), which originally appeared in the brass in the second bar of the intro.

2. In **N7-8** the brass play their rhythm from the first bar of the intro followed by a button, much like **I2-3**.

3. Also in **N7-8** the reeds play an ascending altered pentatonic scale with the following intervals: minor 2nd, major 3rd, major 2nd, minor 3rd, major 2nd, augmented 4th (button). All the ascending 8th notes in **N7** are notes in the Cm7-5: 11, -5, 7, 1, 3, 11. The dramatic jump to the B♮ button sounds pretty wild, since the B♮ is a blue note in A♭ major and the +11 of the F13-9. The ascending scale motif was stated earlier in **A5-7**, **D5-7** and **I7-8**. The tritone leap (to

the button) reminds us of the tritones in **J5-7**.

4. The ascending chromatic line in the first trombone in **N10-12** comes out of the ascending reed line in **E1-3**, where we expect the 7th of the chord to resolve down to the 3rd of the next chord, but instead it resolves chromatically upward.

5. The shoulder chord (E7) in **N11** was seen earlier in **E5**, **H10**, and **M8**.

6. The reeds' ascending diminished triad resolving to a tonic button was used in **F7-8**, **H10-11**, and **M8-9**.

7. The final button in the bones and rhythm section in **N12** is the logical ending following a slew of buttons throughout the piece starting with the 8th bar of the intro.

A Word about Clichés

The following loose ends from the above list are all clichés: #1, 2, 5 and 7.

The great thing about clichés is that everyone knows and loves them. But when used gratuitously, they cheapen a work—much like gratuitous sex and violence in a novel, movie, or TV show. For them to be effective, they need to be *earned*. By that I mean that they need to be integral to the piece—the logical development of the material. Once stated, it is usually very effective to repeat clichés, as evidenced in this chart.

Repetition

So how much repetition is good? That all depends on the material being developed, the genre and the audience. Repetition establishes character, helps the audience to understand the form and makes it easier for the performers to learn their parts and play together.

The Opposite End Of The Bar is, hopefully, a charming little bauble reminiscent of TV variety shows of the 1950s. It's not supposed to be *The Rite Of Spring*. I tried to sneak in as much music as possible without disturbing the commercial appeal of the piece. The result is a surprisingly interesting chart (at least to me) beneath the surface of what could have been business as usual. Is it jazz? Maybe yes, maybe no. But does it accomplish what Paul and I set out to do? I'll leave that up to you.

[Give this chart a final listen (**7-1: Complete Arrangement**). As in many vocal charts I've written throughout my career, I am careful to sneak in dissonances and interesting musical concepts that won't disturb the casual listener and will delight musicians and more sophisticated fans. I could have opted to just give them cake, but I'd rather surprise everyone with a sumptuous and nutritious meal that everyone will enjoy. This is not easy to do, but I like the challenge.]

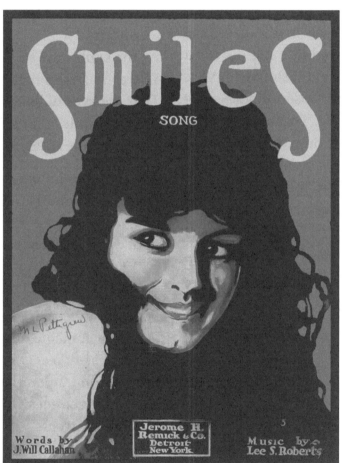

1918 Sheet music cover. Source: Digital Commons at Connecticut College Historic Sheet Music Collection.

8. Smiles

[At www.suchsweetthundermusic.com/pages/cjca2-accompanying-files, listen to **8-1: Complete Arrangement.**]

Did you ever hear Nat Cole's record of *L-O-V-E*? You must have. It was a major hit for Nat back in the day. Like everyone else then, I loved it. I still do. It's a simple little tune with old-fashioned lyrics. The arrangement was by Nelson Riddle—very sparse, but most effective. I wanted to do a similar arrangement, but on a different song. **Smiles** came to mind (it is quite similar musically and lyrically. Being in the public domain (and therefore without any rights issues for recording, publishing, etc.), **Smiles** is kinda old fashioned and familiar. This arrangement is truly an exercise in restraint.

The original form of the song is verse/chorus. Here is what Paul has to say about the words:

"**Smiles** is a lyric that looks both backward and forward. The verse could hardly be more old-fashioned:

Dearie, now I know
Just what makes me love you so,
Just what holds me and enfolds me
In its golden glow.
Dearie, now I see
'Tis each smile so bright and free;
For life's sadness turns to gladness
When you smile on me.

'Dearie;' 'enfolds;' 'golden glow.' This is sentimental operetta stuff, redolent of wrist corsages and fainting couches. But then the chorus is quite straightforward, with an ev-eryday vocabulary that eschews the affected, 'poetic' style of the verse:

There are smiles that make us happy,
There are smiles that make us blue,
There are smiles that steal away the teardrops,
As the sunbeams steal away the dew.
There are smiles that have a tender meaning,
That the eyes of love alone may see,
And the smiles that fill my life with sunshine
Are the smiles that you give to me.

This lyric could easily have been written by Irving Berlin in the '20s. Then comes the second verse, and we are back in the front parlor with our maiden aunts:

Dearie, when you smile,
Everything in life's worthwhile;
Love grows fonder as we wander
Down each magic mile.
Cheery melodies
Seem to float upon the breeze;
Doves are cooing while they're wooing
In the leafy trees.

'Doves are cooing while they're wooing' could not be written or sung after 1920, except in jest. But once we repeat the chorus, we are back in demotic mode, with the possible exception of: 'As the sunbeams steal away the dew,' which is pretty flowery. So in **Smiles** we have a transitional number, one foot in the nineteenth century and one in the twentieth."

Form

For the reasons that Paul states, and my need for the form to resemble Nelson Riddle's, I

SMILES

Lee S. Roberts

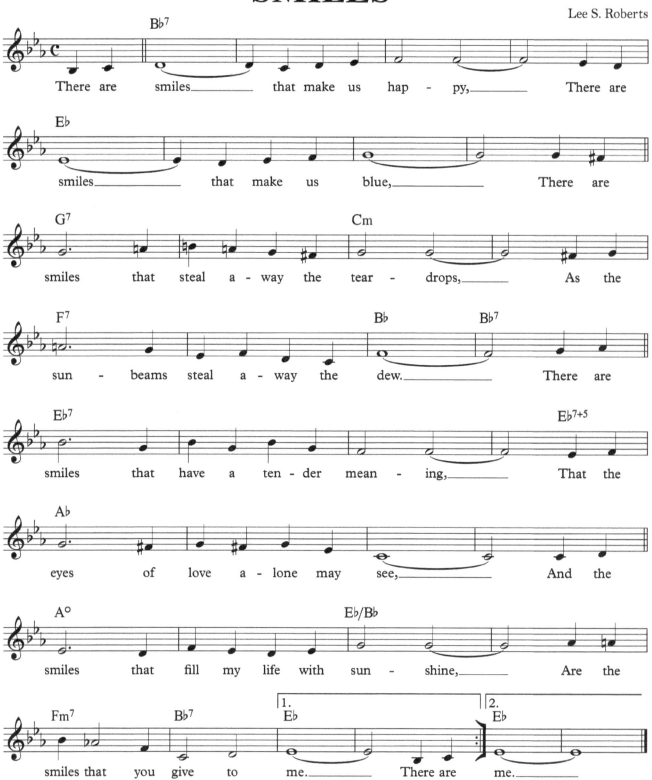

Example 8-1: Lead sheet

omitted the verses altogether. The form of this chart is Intro (four bars), one chorus (vocal), one chorus (trumpet solo) and one chorus with a tag ending (vocal). In order to make each chorus feel fresh, I followed Riddle's example and modulated up a half step each chorus (from E♭ to E to F).

Besides giving the arrangement a lift, modulations sectionalize a chart.

The unusual form of the 32-bar chorus is abb′b″ (see the lead sheet, **Example 8-1**). I can't think of one other song with this through-composed form. Actually, the *b* section is not a true *b*, since it doesn't seem at all like the opposite of *a*. It's really a development of *a*. I'm calling it *b* since the next two sections share the same rhythm as *b*.

We normally expect a bridge on the third 8-bar section. Although the rhythm of this section is identical to that of the previous section *(b)*, alternating minor 3rds in mm. **17-18** along with the *V/IV* chord change (E♭7) almost make it feel like a bridge. The final section of the song uses the same rhythm as the previous two sections for the first four bars, and then introduces a syncopation leading into the final cadence.

Intervals

Alec Wilder, in *American Popular Song: The Great Innovators, 1900-1950*, praised Duke Ellington for his use of wide intervals because they give the music character. 2nds are the glue that holds melodies together. They are pretty ubiquitous and rarely deliver any color or punch. 3rds and 4ths are used fairly often, and therefore don't stand out much. Anything larger grabs our attention.

Establishing a Motif and Developing It

The motif of **Smiles** is the first seven notes of the melody (comprising the entire first phrase), which form an E♭ major scale from the 5th up to the 2nd with a repetition of the 6th and 7th in the middle—all major 2nd intervals, with the exception of the minor 2nd between the leading tone and the tonic.

The second phrase sequences the motif up a step. The third phrase (mm. **8-12**) introduces some chromatics as it modulates to the relative minor (Cm) by way of its dominant (G7). The fourth phrase modulates to the key of the dominant (B♭) through its dominant F7. The fifth and sixth phrases (mm. **16-24**) modulate to the key of the subdominant (A♭). The A° in mm. **25-26** is a pivot chord that functions as a #i° in A♭ and a #iv° in E♭. The rest of the song stays in E♭.

Exploiting Limitations

Smiles begins with 24 consecutive 2nds before introducing a 3rd in measure **14**. The rest of the tune has eleven more 3rds and two 4ths—nothing wider. This sounds like a recipe for boredom, and in fact keeps this song from sounding modern—but there are two saving graces that make it a good, if limited, melody.

1. 10 chromatic notes, 9 of which are blue notes (five F#'s and four A naturals—flat 3rds and flat 5ths). The majority of these chromatics are used as lower neighbors.
2. The interesting succession of basic pitches. Let's boil this tune down to its essentials (see **Example 8-2**):

If we just play the basic pitches and the bass notes, they have a pleasing relationship. If this weren't the melody of the song, the basic pitches would make a good thumb line. Notice how these pitches get filled out and connected

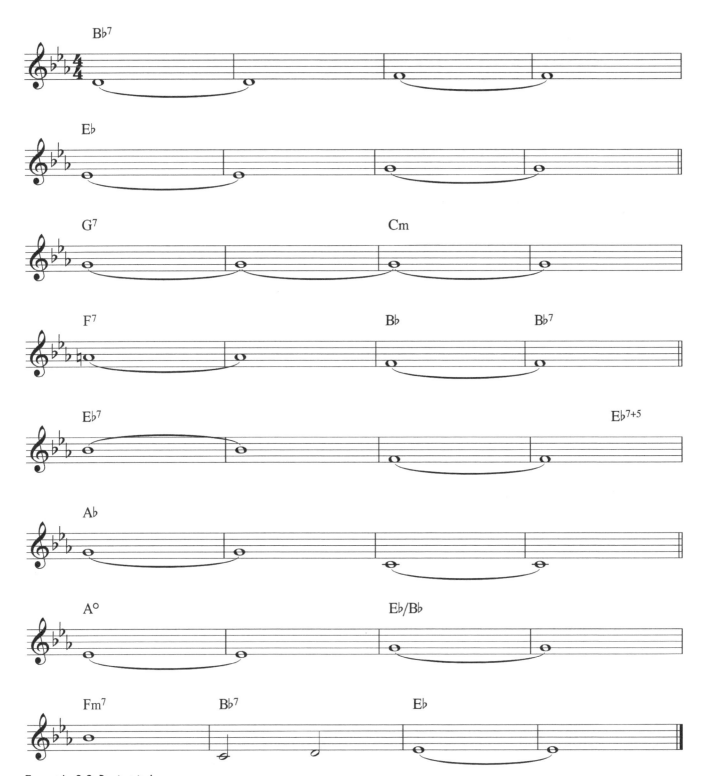

Example 8-2: Basic pitches

in the complete melody—stepwise motion for 13 bars—and then some 3rds are introduced.

Peak Pitches

What about the songwriting "rule" that the highest pitch should only appear once, and that it should be ⅔ to ¾ of the way through the song? B♮ is the highest pitch, and it occurs in measure 10 (way too early). The lowest pitch is C, and it appears 5 times. So much for rules...

Frame from the 1929 Max Fleischer.Screen Songs cartoon *Smiles. Public domain via The Internet Archive.*

Common Practice

Over the years there have been many recordings of this song. Growing up, I heard it many times on TV—probably sung by the inimitable Jimmy Durante, or on *Sing Along With Mitch*, or in a Max Fleischer *Screen Songs* cartoon. Judy Garland sang it in the 1942 movie *For Me And My Gal*.

Although the original sheet music has a G on the downbeat of measure **27**, I'm used to hearing a B♭. This gives us a momentary high point, rather than walking up the scale to the B♭ in m. **25**. Actually, C would have been a better choice, since it would then be the highest note in the song and occur just a bit after the ¾ mark. Theoretically C is better, but I'm so used to hearing B♭ that C sounds wrong to me. So on the third (final) chorus I will add a tag, and take the downbeat of **bar 30** (on the word "give") up the octave, so that it becomes the top vocal note of the chart.

Intro

The functions of an introduction are:

1. Foreshadow the main ideas of the piece.
2. Set the tempo.
3. Establish the groove.

The Vamp or *Ostinato* Intro

A common concept for intros is to set up a repeated pattern or groove that will continue to repeat underneath the melody when it appears at letter **A**. This is mostly used when there is an *ostinato* figure under the melody. Since this song starts with four bars of the dominant before resolving to four bars of the tonic, I devised an ostinato figure for the piano that would work for the tonic (E♭) chord and could be varied slightly to fit the dominant (B♭7). I decided to put the intro on the tonic and then switch to the dominant at **A**, when the vocal enters with the melody.

Melody Chorus

I made sure to avoid the melody notes in the 2-bar ostinato, so that the melody and ostinato would complement each other for the first eight bars of the song. What really makes this ostinato work well for the song is that the intervals of the melody and the ostinato are the same (perfect 4th, minor 3rd, major 2nd), but organized differently.

I use an ascending half step to connect the ostinato patterns (**intro 4, A2, A4, A6**). This is the only other interval found in the melody. I wasn't thinking about any of this when I wrote the ostinato. I was just looking for a catchy, simple, repetitious figure that stayed off the melody pitches. The rest I left up to my subconscious. I varied the ostinato to fit the changes at letter **B**.

Completing the Groove

Although the piano ostinato stops in **B8** to make room for horn backgrounds, the 2-beat bass and hi-hat cymbals continue through the entire chart. Most charts that start in 2, switch to 4 to create more forward motion. However, this chart's charm is its relaxed, relentless 2-beat feel. It never gets hot, nor is it supposed to. I'm a big fan of the Jimmie Lunceford band, which was known for its infectious 2-beat feel. (Actually, I lied. Things do heat up in the New Orleans-style tag in the last few measures of the chart, but we'll look at that later.)

Chord Substitution

Although I'm attracted to chromatic substitute changes, I tried to hold back on this chart for the sake of simplicity. I started with the melody and a simple strong bass part, and where the combination of those two suggested a nice passing chord, I went with it. Passing diminished chords sound particularly good in this style (**B4**, **B6**). I couldn't resist the chromatically descending dominants in **C6**, since they work so well with the melody.

Saxophone Thumb Line

In keeping with the idea of keeping this chart simple and spare, the saxes play a thumb line for the second half of the first chorus. I'll hold off the brass until the next chorus. The thumb line consists mainly of 3rds and 7ths, and avoids the melody and bass notes whenever possible.

[Pause and listen to **8-2: A-E**. There is purposely very little going on in this chorus. Is it enough to hold your interest? It's always surprising to me how effective sparse writing can be.]

Trumpet Solo Chorus

The middle chorus of this chart is a trumpet solo. In the iconic *L-O-V-E* chart by Nelson Riddle, he gives the trumpet only a half chorus. That wouldn't work here because of the through-composed form, combined with the need to modulate up a half step. Besides, I've

got Mike Rodriguez on this recording, and I would feel cheated to hear less than a chorus of his beautiful sound and lyrical approach. Note how both the vocal and saxes cadence on the downbeat of **D7**, turning the spotlight on Mrod for his 2-bar pickup.

Backgrounds

The unison trombones in half plungers play a varied 2-bar riff for the first half of the chorus (**E** and **F**). The idea is to keep the rhythms and pitches as much the same as I can; altering them slightly to fit the chord changes and avoiding predictability. The key interval for the bones is the ascending minor 2nd. As we go along, I invert it a couple of times just for fun, and to keep the players and listeners on their toes.

A Confession

Originally, I planned to have the bones alternate closed and open plungers, but when we read the chart down, all three guys didn't feel comfortable playing it. I also felt that all that movement disrupted the easy groove of the chart, so I asked them to play ½ plungers (no inflections) instead. This worked immediately.

The exchange of knowledge and experience is best when it flows both ways between the arranger/conductor and the players. Respect and appreciation are key.

Sax Riffs

The second half of the trumpet chorus switches backgrounds to unison sax riffs. At this point, I felt like we needed a serious change from the choppy quarter notes and syncopations of the previous trombone background. Since we have a trumpet solo, I'm going to go for the opposite choir and give the background to the saxes. The opposite of choppy quarter notes would be long notes. I'll also syncopate all the notes (*and* of 1, *and* of 4). This fits nicely with the trumpet melody.

Expanding Intervals

One method of developing a motif is to expand its intervals. The vocal melody at **G** has a descending minor 3rd before alternating minor 3rds. The saxes will play all descending intervals starting with a major 3rd in **G1** and an augmented 4th (tritone) in **G3**. **G5-7** reverts to the 2nds of the first 16 bars of the song (just as a reminder of where we've been). Letter **H** gets back to the expansion game: perfect 4th and major 6th. I'll let Mike finish up his solo in the clear before re-introducing Denzal for his final vocal chorus at **I**.

[Let's listen to the chart so far, **8-3: A-I**. Notice how the 2-beat feel is restraining while the half-step modulations create excitement. The key word for this chart is transparency.]

Final Vocal Chorus

Simplify

After the sophisticated 2-bar modulation up a half step, I want to simplify as much as possible for the next 14 bars. The bones play a short one-note syncopated response to the downbeat of each of the first three vocal phrases. They follow that with more syncopated answers before agreeing with the vocal on beat 3 of **J6**. This agreement is short-lived, as the open brass section answers the vocal in **J7-8**.

These bone voicings are the first horn voicings we have heard so far in the entire chart. Everything until now has been unison or solo. As we simplify the melodies and rhythms, we add harmony to create interest. I held off as long as I could. This is an unusually long time

to avoid horn voicings in a big band chart, but it works. In fact it gives the arrangement a very strong character.

Voicing the Three Bones

Since there are only three trombones in our band, and the jazz harmonic language is based on 4-note voicings, one note will need to be omitted in the bone voicings. Roots and 5ths are generally expendable, since the bass has them covered (and in most cases they don't add much color, if any). Aside from the bass, we might also leave out any notes that are being played by another horn section or sung by the vocalist. This should make things relatively easy. Not so fast. I also like the bones to sound complete and feel comfortable in the section, in addition to giving each player a good melody.

Common Tone Riffs

One of the principles of creating riffs is repetition—rhythmic as well as melodic repetition. Sometimes the harmonies change under the riff, so that the pitches in the riff may need to change as well. When this happens, we generally try to keep as many common tones as possible, and move the other voices as little as possible—usually by step. The continuity achieved here may seem insignificant, but if this is not adhered to, the result can be an unfulfilling experience for the players and (subconsciously) the listeners.

Great art integrates thematic material between foreground and background as well as between the most obvious elements and the smallest details. For ensemble players, whole notes and rhythmic figures can be unrewarding to play, unless each note for every player is involved in an interesting vertical and horizontal scheme.

In **I1** I omitted the 5th of the C7 in the bones, opting for the 3rd in the bottom voice. This might have been a close call, since the vocal is singing the E, but I wanted a strong 9th chord sonority. And looking ahead to **I5**, I can just move the entire voicing down a step (diatonically). At **I5** I omitted the root, since both the vocal and the bass cover the root.

Although the notated chord symbol at **J1** is Em7, this really is an A7sus4. I omit the A from the bones, since both the bass and vocal have it. In **J3** I opted for a Dm triad rather than using the 6th. I want to save the 6th for **J5**. In **J4** I'm going to voice the bones beneath the vocal, as if the vocal were the top note in a 4-note bone voicing. The bones play a Dm triad below the vocal's B (the 6th). Since I didn't use the B in the vocal or previous bone voicings in this chorus, it sounds fresh. Besides, I love triads in the bones. It brings out their natural nobility.

The Ab° on beat 3 of **J6** is voiced in open position with a low root in the bottom trombone. All three bones jump down to this voicing, which draws attention to it and signals the imminent change in texture.

6-Note Brass Voicings

The surprise open brass voicings at **J7-8** create immediate heat, and signal that we are taking this baby home. The break in **J8** makes it more dramatic. The Gm7 is voiced as an F triad in the trumpets over a Gm triad in the bones. This resolves to a C9 voicing in the bones (the same voicing we used in **I1**) with the trumpets in 4ths above them. The contrary motion between these two voicings puts a nice accent on this semi-cadence—the three trumpets jump up, Trombones 1 and 2 hold on to their

notes, and the bottom trombone jumps down a 3rd.

The Big Show Biz Finish

In the grandest vaudeville tradition, I'm going to give this sedate chart an unabashed big finale—pull out all the stops. Since we've heard a lot from the bones in the first half of this chorus, I'll give them a rest and have the trumpets add some fire.

Developing the previous trombone plunger *wa's,* in **K1-2**, the trumpets play a standard 2-bar riff with alternating open and closed plungers voiced out in 4-part close harmony with the 9th on top. The riff repeats, making slight adjustments in the 3rd and 4th parts to accommodate the harmony. In **K5** the trumpets keep the G on top, but change the other parts to suit the Bb6. All four trumpets move down a notch for the Fm6. The trumpet rhythm in **K5** squeezes the 2-bar riff into one bar. Rhythmic development like this has a wonderful subliminal effect on the listener.

Sax Thumb Line

The saxes are given a reassuring thumb line in **K1-5**. Their function is to provide continuity and keep the smooth, secure vibe that we've been enjoying throughout the chart. They play all 7ths and 3rds, except for the chromatic C# in **K4** leading to the D in **K5** (the 3rd of Bb). The C# is the +5 of the F9 chord. The whole tone effect that this chord gives (its five notes contain five of the six notes of the F whole tone scale—omitting only B♮) has a quaint quality reminiscent of 1920s jazz, which seems perfectly suited to this arrangement.

Call-and-Response

The saxes respond to the **K5** trumpet figure a bar later, with a similarly 4-part close voiced rhythmic figure. They take the trumpet rhythm of **K5** and displace them by a beat—starting on the downbeat instead of on beat 2, and syncopating the final note, rather than putting it on the beat.

The saxes also appear to be the opposite of the trumpets in the tonal color of their instruments (brass vs. reeds) and register (more than an octave below). Also opposite from the trumpets, the saxes play chromatically descending 9th chords, rather than repeating their voicings.

The trumpets then answer the saxes in **K7** with a 3-note development of the riff (retrograde of the trumpet figure in **K5** with the last note truncated), but this time they are open and joined by two trombones. Trumpet 2 and Trombone 1 are omitted. They will be joining the clarinet and bari sax in **L12** for the New Orleans ending.

5-Part Brass Voicings

We've got three brass notes in **K7**. The lead trumpet plays the major 7th, 3rd and major 7th of the B♭ chord, which reminds us of all the 3rds and 7ths that the saxes played in their thumb line in **K1-5**. I'll voice the major 7ths as B♭maj7 chords and use a B7 as the sandwich chord. This gives us contrary motion between the bottom trombone and all the other horns. Also the D on top makes the +9 of the B7, an interesting tension. +9 chords supply some blues feeling, which was implied by the plungers and the use of melodic blue notes throughout the chart.

I'm going to voice both B♭maj7 chords the same for continuity. This voicing has an interesting intervallic relationship: the two bones are in 5ths, as are the top two trumpets. The fourth trumpet is a 5th above the top trombone and a major 2nd below Trumpet 3. Perfect 5ths and major 2nds connote cool, non-sensual emotion, while the major 7th interval between the outer voices (Trumpet 1 and Trombone 3) is somewhat abrasive and volatile. Overall, this voicing has a placid feeling.

In contrast the B7 chord is highly volatile with its tritone (3rd and 7th) and major 7th between the 3rd and +9. This B7 chord is voiced with an upper structure triad—D major triad in the trumpets over B and D# (root and 3rd of a B7) in the bones. This sexy chord demands resolution. I love the juxtaposition of cool/hot/cool.

The Set-up

Rather than continuing to pound away to the finish, I'm going to bring the volume down for the next 10 bars. I'll give the trumpets a rest (and give our ears a rest from them as well), so that I can save all my big guns for the big vaudeville tag.

One of the key elements of mature performing art is pacing.

So often I hear bands that only play loud, or bands that only play dense, dissonant voicings. Then there are bands that only play odd rhythms, or those with unusual instrumental combinations. At the risk of seeming too graphic, this is like an immature lover whose only thought is to race to the finish line and then ask, panting, "That was great, wasn't it?"

As in sex, one of the most rewarding moments can be when everything is building to a climax and suddenly we lower the intensity and take a moment to savor the feeling that the big finish is on its way. As with most things in life, the anticipation can be as much fun as the pay-off.

Start Simple and Add

Letter **L** starts with unison saxes in 8th notes using diatonic upper neighbors and chromatic lower neighbors. On 4 *and* of **L1** they spread out into an E7+5 voicing in Drop 2. On 3 *and* of **L3** they spread out into an E♭13 voicing in Drop 2 and follow with a D9 voicing in close position.

Interval Expansion and Contraction

Letters **G** and **H** introduced the developmental technique of interval expansion. I'm going to follow up on that in the saxes at **L**, starting with major 2nds, then minor 2nds (interval contraction), followed by a jump up of a minor 7th. The next figure (**L3-4**) uses a minor 2nd and then jumps up a major 7th before descending a minor 6th. **L5** repeats unison Ds (as contracted as we can get) before perfect 5ths and a diminished 5th. **L7-8** continues with the repeated pitches, sequenced a step lower, before jumping up a minor 7th.

Trombone Contrapuntal Punches

The bones enter in **L4**, voiced with the vocal for two beats before acting on their own. The Gm7 in **L5** is voiced as a Gm triad. The D7 chord has the vocal on the +5, so the bones play the tried-and-true 3, 7, +9 voicing with a fall-off (for blues expression). In **L6** the bones switch to voicings with roots on the bottom in root, 7th, 3rd voicings. Then it's back to rootless voicings in **L7-8**, with a tritone between the two bottom voices. On beat 4 and

4 *and*, the bones revert to rooted voicings in 1, 7, 3 position to put a solid finish to this section. I was careful to avoid unison pitches and rhythms between the saxes and bones. The result is that they start building intensity without much volume.

Clearing the Palate, and then Pulling Out All the Stops

L9 has all the horns resting to clear the palate. Then the brass develop the trumpet rhythms of letter **K**. This time they are open rather than in plungers. The saxes play a thumb line in **L10-11** before joining the unison brass for a figure that combines the previous brass figure and the sax figures in **L5-8**. Since the saxes and brass are in unison, I am able to add the clarinet, bari, Trumpet 2 and Trombone 1 in counterpoint using open 4-part harmony.

I wanted this to sound like New Orleans music, where the trumpet has the lead, but the clarinet is voiced above him in his screaming register. Each of the four parts has a strong melody and is in a strong register. I added the bari to the traditional New Orleans front line (clarinet, trumpet, trombone) so that I could write 4-part harmony with a little more weight and harmonic color.

[Listen again to **8-1: Complete Arrangement**. Does it maintain interest while building throughout? Does the chart help to sell the words?]

1-Frank Sinatra and Peggy Lee. 2-Doris Day. 3-Joe Williams. 4-Sammy Davis, Jr. 5-Ella Fitzgerald (shown with Dizzy Gillespie, Ray Brown in background). 6-Cab Calloway. 7-Dinah Washington. 8-Nat "King" Cole. 9-Jon Hendricks. 10-Dean Martin, Judy Garland and Frank Sinatra. 11-Anita O'Day (shown with Paul Weston and Stan Kenton). 12-Billie Holiday. 13-Johnny Mercer. 14-Ethel Waters. 15-Sarah Vaughan. 16-Madeline Peyroux. 17-Thomas "Fats" Waller.

Image credits: 1-Photo by Kate Gabrielle. Classic Film Scans, Creative Commons license. 2, 5-6, 8, 11-15, 17- William P. Gottlieb Jazz Collection, Library of Congress, public domain. 3-Photo by Brian McMillen, brianmcmillen@hotmail.com, Creative Commons via Wikipedia. 4, 7-Creative Commons license via Wikipedia. 10-CBS Television, Creative Commons via Wikipedia. 16-Photo by Borya, Creative Commons via Wikipedia.

Those Lips, Those Eyes

Elizabeth Taylor, mid-1950s. Public domain via Wikipedia.

9. Those Lips, Those Eyes

[At www.suchsweetthundermusic.com/pages/cjca2-accompanying-files, listen to **9-1: Complete Arrangement.**]

I started with the title, which came from the movie of the same name. In it, Frank Langella plays a Broadway matinee idol whose career is slumping, forcing him to play summer stock. His ability on stage is surpassed only by his prowess at seducing women. His stock line, which he uses to great success, is "Those lips! Those eyes!" It's corny, but it works, especially on younger, less experienced women. Warning: The following analysis is rated PG and is intended for adults. No animals were injured in the writing of this chapter.

I wrote the song with the title in mind and gave it to Paul, who ran with the title and, in typical Larry Hart fashion, effortlessly filled out the story in minutes. It took me about a half hour to write the song and then maybe six hours to arrange it. I don't remember either Paul or me having to make any changes to accommodate each other's work, although I did ask him to add lyrics to the tag at the end of the chart. He didn't even have to think about that. I played it for him once, and he told me the words. Sometimes songs come easily, especially when we are inspired.

This is one of those songs where you can't forget the title, since it comes near the beginning and is repeated at the end. Notice how the consonant and vowel sounds fit the melody's long and short notes as well as high and low notes (see **Examples 9-1** and **9-2**, next page). Not only is this song easy to sing, it's also fun.

The entire range of the tune is a major 10th, which is pretty standard. This makes it possible to modulate up a half step and still have a narrow enough range to suit Denzal's voice. The highest note, *ti* (C in the key of Db) occurs as a dotted quarter note in bar **4** and then repeats in the second a section in bar **12**. The surprise comes in the third measure of the final *a* section when the C appears two bars earlier than before and is held for six beats—creating a satisfying climax, even though we have heard this note twice previously. It doesn't hurt that the long note starts as the interesting 13th of the Eb7 chord. As we hold out the note, the band moves up the scale: Eb7, Fm7, F#°, followed by Gm7-5.

The form of the song is *aaba'*. The syncopated pickup dotted quarter followed by a quarter note downbeat a minor 3rd below *(sol mi)* is our motif. It repeats and then is altered by holding out the downbeat in bar **3** for six beats. The pickup to bar **5** sequences our motif a 3rd above *(ti sol)*—thus expanding the minor 3rd to a major 3rd.

Shades of Louis Jordan

Two things differentiate this tune from thousands of others. The first is the switch to a shuffle feel on the bridge. That suggested itself to me because of the chord changes at letter **C**: IV, I, IV, I (basically). It was a typical bridge on a number of Louis Jordan records, so it seemed fitting to also borrow his shuffle feel. This provides a nice contrast to the 2-beat feel on the *a* sections.

BASIC LEAD SHEET

THOSE LIPS, THOSE EYES

Berger/Mendenhall

Example 9-1: Basic lead sheet   © 2010 Such Sweet Thunder

FINAL LEAD SHEET

THOSE LIPS, THOSE EYES

Berger/Mendenhall

Example 9-2: Final lead sheet

© 2010 Such Sweet Thunder

Chromatic Inversion

The other distinguishing factor in this tune is the third *a* section. I've labeled it *a'*, since the melody is an inverted form of the original *a* section. The rhythms are the same, but the melody ascends chromatically, rather than descending by a third. I can't think of any other song that does this; nevertheless, it feels natural.

Diatonicism with Blue Notes

Like most of the American Songbook, this tune is almost completely diatonic. Of the 64 melody notes in the 32-bar form, there are only seven accidentals—six of them blue notes (five flat 3rds and one flat 5th). The remaining chromatic is the flat 6th in **C5** (the chromatic upper neighbor to the following note). Diatonic and blue note melodies are easy to hear and sing. The blue notes give the feeling of the blues—especially when the flat 3rd (F♭) forms the 7th of the *IV* chord (G♭7) on the bridge.

Louis Jordan at the Paramount in New York City, 1946. Photo by William P. Gottlieb. Source: Library of Congress.

Chord Progression

Basically, this song shares the common *Exactly Like You* and *Take the A Train* chord progression for the *a* sections. I wrote the melody first, without even thinking about chords. After the melody was finished, I knew immediately what the basic chords were, and then proceeded to dress up the melody with chords that would make the melody sound more sophisticated and be more fun to play.

I generally work out the bass line against the melody before filling in the inner voices by using my intuition on when to use diatonic chords and when to spice things up with secondary dominants and chromatic chords. I'm always conscious of how the melody notes relate to the bass.

One melody/bass concern is balancing parallel, contrary, and oblique motion. If we boil down the melody to its most basic pitches, we have 4 bars of F, 1 bar of A♭, 1 bar of B♭ and 2 bars of F. Over the static F of the first 4 bars, I started with 2 bars of chromatically descending dominant 7ths followed by 2 bars of ascending diatonics with a passing diminished. The minor *ii V* into Fm sets up a reversal of the previous diatonic/diminished progression—this time descending from *iii biii⁰ ii V I*.

Tension and Release

These are all common progressions, but when they make tensions and altered tensions of the melody notes, they sound fresh. In the first *a* section we have eight chord tones in the melody and eight tensions, as compared to the bridge, which has 16 chord tones and three tensions. I love dissonant melodies as much as the next guy, but if the music sounds good to me with simpler relationships, I'll go for simplicity. Since bridges need to be oppo-

THOSE LIPS, THOSE EYES

site in nature to the *a* sections, the simplicity of the bridge balances the complexity of the *a* sections.

What sounds good to me?

Over a period of many years, I have become more and more sensitive to the balance of details, so that when I speak the language of jazz, I sound like a native and not a foreigner with an accent, or someone imitating a native. Some of these choices are artistic and some are specific to jazz. My goal is to be both authentic and artistic.

Form

The overall form for this chart is:

Key of D♭: 6½ -bar Intro, 32-bar vocal chorus (*aaba'*), 32-bar chorus solos (tenor/trumpet),

Key of D: 32-bar vocal chorus + 2-bar tag and 4-bar coda.

With the exception of the intro, this is standard song form treatment. The vocal states the melody, the soloists and band develop it, and the vocal comes back to recap it, extending the last few bars to finish the story and create a feeling of finality. The modulation up a half step for the last vocal chorus is also standard. It provides a needed lift.

The Introduction

Normally intros are 2, 4 or 8 bars long. This one has an odd length, but it feels natural. In an intro, we want to state the motif or motifs of the piece, but in a way that doesn't give away the story—just make the melody sound familiar to a certain extent. So, what's with the 2/4 bar? Certainly, I could have added six beats before the 2/4 bar, which would have made the intro the usual 8 bars, but I didn't. Why not?

For one thing, I've already made my statement, and it is time to move on. No need to add extra beats of filler. But more importantly, the intro is a tease. You know how, at the beginning of Beethoven's *Fifth Symphony*, we don't know if those three pickup notes are eighth notes or a triplet? I'm playing a similar game here. Our motif of a syncopated dotted quarter followed by a quarter note on the beat is central not only to the song, but the entire arrangement.

If you know this song, then you know that the descending minor 3rd dotted quarter is a pick-up occurring on the *and* of 3. This chart starts with a prank played on the listener. Instead of the dotted quarter being on 3-*and*, I introduce it two beats earlier in measure **1**. Measure **2** shortens the note values to 8th notes, first starting on beat 2 and then the *and* of 3. Now we are confused.

I'm going to run with those 8th notes and expand them in bars **3** and **4** in the saxes, where the naturally accented top D♭ to C in both measures also squeezes the melodic interval from a minor 3rd to a minor 2nd. This occurs on the *and* of 2 in both measures.

Bars **5-6** in the trombones, bari sax and bass continue the descending minor 2nd while re-instating the dotted quarter motif, only this time it is followed by a long note. Oh, and one other thing—it occurs on the downbeat of the bar. The piano answers in double octaves echoing the sax 8th note pattern, only this time starting 2 beats later on the *and* of 3 with the top D♭'s on the *and* of 4 and the *and* of 2.

So where are we? All of a sudden the saxes, bass and vocal come in on the *and* of 1 of bar **7** with the first note of the song, thus leading us to believe that the motif is in the first half of the bar—as it was in measure **1**. But, surprise!

This first melody note comes in a 2/4 bar and establishes it as a pickup. Pretty tricky, no?

If that isn't enough, what key are we in?

The melody starts *sol mi* (A♭ F), but the lead trumpet in the first two bars of the intro keeps hammering B♭ G, suggesting *sol mi* a whole step higher (the key of E♭?). The use of dominant chords to harmonize both notes and their repetition in the next measure lead us to suspect that we are no longer in Kansas or the key of E♭. The bitonal voicings (B♭/D7 and A7/G7) further obscure the tonality. In bars **3-4** the saxes suggest E♭7. That could be the dominant in A♭ or a *V/V* in D♭. Let's see.

The E9 to E♭9 in bars **5-6** with the piano suggesting E♭7 keeps us in suspense. But then, aha! The vocal, saxes and bass slide down a half step to a D9+11 (the tritone sub of A♭7). Now we know that we are indeed in the key of D♭ and, sure enough, on the downbeat of letter **A**, we get our D♭ chord. The deception is over, at least for now.

But why all the deception?

What's the title of the song? What does it refer to? I hope I'm not going to give away any mating secrets, but when I was young, girls would say no, and boys would use subtle ways to convince them, to get a kiss and hopefully more. When I became a man, things got a little easier as women became more empowered, but basically, the same seduction game went on. I suppose this sounds silly, since women enjoy intimacy and sex as much as men. But, since men don't get pregnant and women do, we have this biological game ingrained in our psyches before we even know what a psyche is. The point of all of this is that the man needs to be clever to disarm his covertly willing prey.

This mating ritual is the source of countless stories, novels, plays and songs going back to the beginning of the animal kingdom. The successful Romeo knows how to convince his Juliet that she desires him as much as he desires her. And maybe she does, but she can't let on, or that would ruin the game. One thing I know about sex is that it is much more fun when there is some suspense. A negligee is so much more provocative than, "Let's have sex."

Don't Forget to Laugh

Another thing about sex is that it is the source of much humor. Every generation tells its own jokes on the subject. Seduction with humor can be most effective. When we tell a joke, we tease the audience. And since teasing is a large part of sex, there is plenty of overlap.

And so, by the time we get to the downbeat at **A**, we have a pretty good idea what this chart is all about and how clever the protagonist is at the game. It's no coincidence that Paul and I have chosen obvious clichés in both the lyrics and the music. We want you to enjoy how we can be so obvious and still be convincing. The key to the use of clichés is to earn them. We are not being gratuitous. Sex and humor are serious business with us.

The Head

Following our mazelike introduction, the melody chorus is presented in a straightforward manner. The *a* sections repeat to establish stability. The first time around the bones and bari answer the vocal with syncopated pecks on the *and* of 3 and then switch to the *ands* of 1 and 3, while the vocal holds out his long note. The bones play typical 3-note piano left hand voicings, and the bari functions as a bass trombone and anchors them on the roots of the chords. Each dominant 7th voicing puts Trombones 2 and 3 on the 3rd and 7th of each chord while Trombone 1 gets the +9s and 13th. On the Fm7 the lower bones stick with 3rd and 7th and the lead gets the 11th. Since the vocal is holding out an F, we don't really need another tension in the F#° chord, so the bones and bari fan out into a plain old Drop 2 and 4 voicing. While all this is going on, the bass and drums are playing in 2, which has a relaxed, coy feel.

Changing the Orchestration and Texture

The horn rebuttals switch over to the saxes in measures **A5-6**. They are voiced in open 5-part harmony with the bari continuing on the roots. Each voicing has a 9th in it to supply tension and obscure our sneaky motives (and motifs). Notice how they mostly move by 3rds, with the lead alto moving up and down by major 3rds imitating the vocal's descending major 3rd from bar **A4-5**.

While the vocalist holds out his F in A7, the brass answer in 7-part harmony for the turnaround. In general when I write for the brass section, I like to give each player his own pitch. There are some exceptions, but this is the sound that I strive for. In this spot the brass alternate 7-part upper structure triads with unison tonics for the first four notes. The tonics are played as ghost notes, so I give them less weight with the unisons.

Stacking 3rds

For the B7 and B♭7 the voicings are stacked 3rds. Although this is very basic, it sounds good in brass. The result is D♭/B7 and C/B♭7. I could have planed down one more time for the A7, but the +11 in the 2nd Trumpet didn't feel right—too much parallel motion—predictable. I kept everyone else moving chromatically

down, but put the 3rd in the 2nd Trumpet (doubling the 2nd Trombone at the octave).

The E♭m7 has root/5th on the bottom and then is voiced up in 3rds starting with the minor 3rd in the lead trombone. This voicing has a D♭ triad in the top 3 trumpets over an E♭m7. The final A♭7-9 voicing is F/A♭7. For these two bars I have the bass and drums go into 4 (bass alternating roots and -5's) and then catch the rhythms of the brass and sax voicings—the saxes playing a sonorous D7+9 voiced 1, 5, 3, 7, +9 below the vocal. D7 is the tritone sub of the dominant (A♭7).

When arranging turnarounds, rather than just writing clichés or generic filler that merely addresses the chord changes, it is more effective to incorporate a central motif of the piece. By doing so you create unity, and at the same time keep the chart focused on developing your motifs. In this case, if we ignore the repeated tonic D♭'s, the lead trumpet line descends chromatically (like the saxophone thumb line and the accompanying bass line) and more importantly ends with the all-important descending minor 3rd motif *(sol mi)*.

Adding a Thumb Line on the Repeat

For the repeat of the *a* section, it is customary to add an element, both to surprise the listener and to keep the arrangement building. In this case, since the bones are answering the vocal with harmonized short pecks, I give the saxes a thumb line. These stepwise descending unison half notes are like glue—they bind everything together without being obtrusive.

Notice the *p* dynamic. This is essential. You want the saxes to be way under the vocal, and not compete with it in any way. Actually the saxes only descend for the first two measures (following the roots of the descending chords).

Then they turn around and start ascending with the ascending bass notes in bars **A3-4**.

A5 is the same as the first time around. **A9** uses our rhythmic motif, but displaced forward by two beats. The pitches are different, but the lead alto line keeps the descending shape—transforming it slightly (a descending major 2nd instead of a minor 3rd).

The following *tutti* figure begins with the same descending major 2nd *(la sol)* and then returns to the descending minor 3rd motif—this time from the blue note flat 3rd to the tonic. Before we get to the tonic a lower B♭ *(la)* is inserted. This note then resolves up a minor 3rd to the final tonic D♭, thus giving us a descending and an ascending minor 3rd cadence. These consonant 4-part close *tutti* voicings are welcome relief from the more dissonant 5-part sax voicings.

The unison bones answer the *tutti* with a dominant pedal (A♭) that signals the entrance of a new section. It serves as both a divider and a connector between sections.

Shifting Gears for the Bridge

For a bridge to be effective, it needs to be as different as possible from the *a* section of the song while still being constructed from the same building blocks. In this case, the minor 3rd motif is the similarity. By shifting where the minor 3rd falls in the scale and its direction, we have disguised it sufficiently. The ascending minor 3rd pickup to downbeat D♭ to F♭ in the vocal line sets the tone for these eight bars. That F♭ is the blue note flat 3rd and instantly removes us from the diatonic/chromatic *a* section to the land of the blues. The answering phrase in the vocal reasserts the major 3rd.

This is so gratifying that we repeat this pattern in the second half of the bridge, and solidify the major tonality by adding the chromatic 4, #4, 5 finish. This chromatic pattern reminds us of our descending bass line and sax thumb line from the *a* section.

So that's what's the same as the *a* section. Now let's examine what is different.

The most noticeable element is the shift from 2-beat to 4/4 shuffle. **B1-2** and **B5-6** use the standard boogie-woogie bass line that every kid my age learned to play on the piano. This works perfectly for the G♭7, but in order to accommodate the diatonic/chromatic chords in **B3-4** and **B7-8**, I just stick to the roots of each chord. In true Louis Jordan or Jan Savitt shuffle style, the pianist doubles the bass notes in his left hand and plays chord voicings on the *ands* of each beat in his right hand. In addition to feeling uplifting, this groove inserts a degree of levity into the proceedings.

The unison saxes first mock the vocal with tritones (the happy 6th to the blue flat 3rd) and then resolve to perfect intervals by moving the blue flat 3rd up to the natural 3rds. The tritones return for the repeat of the E♭7 in **B5-6**. The bari is *tacet*. I could have doubled him an octave below, but I wanted a lighter sound,

Throughout the bridge, the bones answer both the vocal and the saxes, avoiding their rhythms and pitches as much as possible. This gives each section a separate and distinct character, creating both conflict and complementary interaction.

Natural Instrumental Characteristics

In general, reeds are best at legato passages, and brass excel at playing punchy rhythms.

That is not to say that they are limited to those functions, but these are their natural assets. To use my favorite baseball analogy, a pitcher gets to the major leagues on the strength of his 100-mile per hour fastball, but quickly learns that developing a breaking ball gives his delivery variety and unpredictability. A steady diet of fastballs becomes hittable, no matter how fast, because the batter knows what's coming.

With three trombones, the safe, tried and true voicing technique is to give the second and third bones the 3rds and 7ths of each chord, leaving the lead trombonist with 9ths, 13ths and their alterations. This is basically what most post-1950 pianists play in their left hands.

This can become formulaic, and also can contain some of the same pitches that the vocal and saxes are covering, thus lessening the individuality that we are trying to create between sections. Some duplication may be necessary, as there are only so many notes available in each chord, but I try to keep it to a minimum while creating good melodic lines for each player. Although the vertical voicings seem to be of obvious importance, sitting inside a section, the melodic nature of your own part determines how you approach playing it and ultimately affects how natural the passage sounds to the listener.

Let's take a look at the bones on the bridge.

I have either omitted the saxophone note or the vocal note from the trombone voicings, avoiding the more prominent of the two. In **B1-2** and **5-6** the saxes hold out B♭'s, so this would be a good note to avoid. Hence the 3rd-less voicing in the bones. I took a different tact in **B3-4** and had the bones and vocal

act as a section, creating 4-part close voicings between them. Denzal's vocal sounds an octave below where written, but I really don't care about that. I'm just looking for combined 4-part harmony. The same goes for **B7**.

The brass answer in **B8** is different—there are no saxes or vocal, and we have 7 brass available. The E9+11 chord is built up in 3rds and resolves down a step to the E♭m11—except for the lead trumpet, who resolves up a step to the root, creating contrary motion. Employing contrary motion for cadences gives a feeling of arrival to a point of rest, which is what we want to establish in a cadence.

Adding the trumpets at this point wraps a bow around this package. The bass and drums join the brass for emphasis. Notice that the trumpets are in the middle register. I'm going to save any upper register trumpet notes for the next phrase, when I need that excitement. I don't want to overdo that and have them lose their impact.

Dealing with the Final *a* Section

The first two *a* sections of the head are nearly identical, leading us to expect the same for the return of a at Letter C. The rhythm of the melody, the chords and the 2-beat feel are the same, but the melody is inverted and squeezed a bit (from descending minor 3rds to ascending minor 2nds). I've changed the texture of the horn accompaniment completely to call-and-response using *tutti* voicings for 2 bars and then expanding to full ensemble voicings in **C3-4**.

The 1-bar horn responses voiced in 4-part close *tutti* voicings have the bones and saxes an octave below the trumpets. They answer the vocal by shouting back Denzal's rhythms, but inverted melodically. Where the vocal intervals are squeezed, the brass answers hark back to the vocal motif at **A**, but expanding the intervals from descending minor 3rds to descending perfect 5ths, which are more suitable for final cadences because of the added stability.

C3-4 has the vocal melody reach up to a C *(ti)*, which is the highest note of the song and, not coincidentally, the climax. It's especially effective in that following the descending minor 3rds, we have an ascending major 3rd. The combination of the surprising change in direction and the slightly larger interval would be enough to satisfy us, but there is one more relationship at work here. The minor 3rds resolving to major 3rds ties this *a* section to the bridge, in which the same minor/major relationship is played out intervallically, but on different pitches.

All the horns answer the vocal high note with repeated voicings moving up the scale diatonically with a passing chromatic diminished chord (F#o). The trumpet lead line goes chromatically up from the +11 on the Eb13 to the 11 on the Fm9 to the 11 on the F#o to the 11 on the Gm9-5. The trumpets are voiced in close position with the trombones directly beneath them and the saxes in open root position chords on the bottom. This is the climax of the chart so far. We feel gratified to hear the lead trumpet inch up to the high C, which matches the previous note in the vocal.

Settling Down and Transitioning into Solos

In **C5** the brass drop out and the saxes play a decorated thumb line for a bar before supporting the vocal with a standard *ii V*. Note that the tenor rests for these 2 bars to prepare for his upcoming solo. The saxes are voiced in

spread chords with the roots in the bari. I used the 9th instead of the 5th on the Ebm7, since the Bb appears in the vocal. Similarly, the 13th is in the vocal on the Ab13-9, so I was able to place a flat 9th in the 2nd Alto part. Notice the wide melodic intervals in the saxes in answer to the previous scale-wise movement in **C3-4**. Opposites feel rewarding.

The Turnaround

When I was 14 my brother bought me the Count Basie Decca recordings. I listened to them obsessively. Lester Young became my hero. I think I can still sing every one of his solos. Prez did this interesting thing; he would often start his solo 1 or 2 bars early and give us a preview. That's what is happening here over the turnaround. Dan starts his tenor solo while the brass play syncopated mid-register voicings in 6-part harmony.

Essentially, these are 5-part voicings with added roots in the bottom trombone. The -9 is hidden in the 1st Trombone on the Bb7+5 chord. The next 2 chords use upper structure triads in the trumpets—Db/Ebm7 and E/D7. The lower dynamic of **C5-8** signals that the

Lester Young soloing at the Spotlite, New York, 1946. Photo by William P. Gottlieb. Source: Library of Congress.

vocal is over for now and we are moving into the instrumental solo section of the chart.

[Let's listen to the chart up to this point, **9-2: A-D**. Is the story clear? Does the chart help to flesh out our protagonist's personality? Does the humor of the lyrics come across? Are the horns sufficiently integral to the arrangement? Do we want to stick around and find out how this story turns out?]

Instrumental Solos

Sandwiched between the two vocal choruses is a chorus of instrumental solos split equally between tenor sax and trumpet. You probably noticed that Trumpet 3 is *tacet* in **C7-8**. The same 6-part brass voicings continue behind the tenor in **D** right up to Trumpet 3's solo entrance at **E**. For the sake of consistency, Trumpet 3 is *tacet* for the entire 16 bars. In order to achieve maximum color differentiation between the soloist and background, I stay with the brass throughout the saxophone solo, and then switch to sax backgrounds for the trumpet solo.

The brass at **D** continue in the same manner as the previous 2 measures, both in their syncopated rhythms (*and* of 2/*and* of 4) and their open voicings with the trumpets (playing mostly tensions, altered tensions and upper structure triads) and the bottom trombone on roots. The one rootless voicing occurs on the *and* of 4 of **D2**, where the bottom trombone plays the 3rd of the E♭9 chord thereby allowing the 4th Trumpet to play the +11.

Oblique Motion

Although the 1st Trumpet and 1st Trombone play octave F's (the 9th) in **D2-5**, the trombone moves down in oblique motion for the next chord. Similarly, Trumpet 2 holds out a C

in **D3** and resolves upward to a D on the next measure. Trombone 2 plays D♭, then plays the octave doubling C in the second half of the bar, and holds the C over into the next bar while the trumpet moves off the C upwardly to the D. I find these kinds of mirror voicings interesting to listen to and perhaps even more interesting to play.

The Long and Short of It

Although the textures and orchestration at **D** are similar in many ways to the preceding two bars, they differ greatly in a very important way—long and short. This immediately signals a new section to the listener and says, "Don't be fooled by the tenor starting 2 bars before the new chorus. We are still in a 32-bar chorus form." Eventually the short brass pecks return to the longer syncopated voicings similar to **C7-8**, making the entire 18 bars feel of one piece.

Establishing an Opposite Solo

Trumpet 3 takes over the solo chores in **E** and **F** with sax backgrounds. The saxes start with a variation of the bridge melody in octave unison (altos up and tenor/bari down), and switch to 4-part open voicings with roots in the bari. The added trills are a special effect idiomatic to reed instruments that is especially effective in conjunction with a diminuendo. Notice that I didn't go into the shuffle for this bridge as I did in the head. Also the rhythm section is in 4/4 for this chorus, rather than the 2-beat rhythm from the previous a sections.

Letter **F** lets the trumpet solo in the clear for 8 bars. This natural diminuendo cleanses our palate, making way for the return of the vocal for his final chorus.

[Let's listen to **9-3: D–G**. Is it clear who is soloing and who has the background? Do we still hear the character of the piece—is the story continuing without the singer's words? Is it time to move on and bring back the singer for his final chorus?]

Recapitulation

Denzal comes back for his final chorus at **G**. I felt that we could use a lift at this point, so I had the rhythm section start a 2-bar modulation in **F7-8**. In order to modulate up a half step to D major, I used chromatically descending dominant 7th chords (two beats per change) starting in measure **F7**. The modulation starts with G♭7, which just happens to be the first bar of the bridge from our previous two choruses. Because of that, it feels natural and integral. Similarly, the chromatically descending dominant 7ths follow the pattern of the first 2 bars of the previous *a* sections. Although there are no melodic or rhythmic motifs at work here, the familiarity of the harmonies and harmonic rhythm do much to make a smooth transition. I'll leave the rest up to the soloist and pianist. I think I've given them enough hints that they should know what to do.

Call-and-Response

Since the first statement of the melody at letter **A** uses call-and-response between the vocal and the trombones, and then between the vocal and the *tutti* horns at **C**, I don't want to repeat that relationship. I could either not respond to the vocal, or reverse the order of call-and-response. Reversing the order appeals to me, since I won't need to create new material to create an opposite effect.

The saxes and vocal reverse roles starting with the pickup to **G1**. The saxes state the melody of the song from **F8-G3** with the vocal answering a half beat later, and then the saxes coming back a half beat after the vocal—and so on in simplified *stretto* fashion. The listener has no trouble telling the vocal apart from the saxes, due to their different tone color, use of words and texture—the saxes being in 5-part harmony.

The vocal gets back to the original melody at the end of **G2**. The saxes reverse the dotted quarter pattern in **G3** and jump down on the *and* of 2 for an open voicing with the root in the bari. After resting six beats, the saxes return, changing their dynamic and texture to a *p* unison thumb line that moves parallel with the bass in 10ths.

Plunger Muted Brass Turnaround

Just as the saxes went from loud to soft in letter **G**, the brass follow suit, only in a more dramatic fashion—a loud plunger *wah* followed by five soft *doo-wahs* in 6-part harmony. The lead trumpet repeats B's while the 5 parts below descend chromatically, thus forming interesting oblique motion.

The repeat of letter **G** is essentially the same as the first time, but with different words, until we get to the second ending. Where this spot was harmonized with a tonic 6th chord in the first two choruses, this time around I used a D13+11 (*V/V*). This feels bluesy and pulls us toward the subdominant first chord of the bridge. The saxes provide the interesting harmony which the octave unison brass arpeggiate up the tonic triad after they get over their initial stutter. Those stuttering repeated D's refer back to the repeated lead trumpet B's in **G7-8**.

The Final Bridge

We are too far along in the chart to be introducing new material. It's time to tie up some loose ends. It would be fun to put together a bunch of disparate elements from earlier in the chart. Here they are:

- The shuffle rhythm with the boogie-woogie bass line (**H1-8**).
- 5-part open sax voicings descending chromatically (**H8**).
- Oblique motion combined with 5-part open sax voicings descending chromatically (**G10, H4**).
- Call-and-response (between brass and saxes (**H1-8**).
- Plunger muted doo-wahs in the brass (**H1-2, 5-6**).
- Unison sax lines (**H3-4, 7-9**).

Using Distinct Instrumental Registers To Your Advantage

Every time we write a figure, it conveys a message. It's part of the story. Sometimes it's the hero slaying the dragon; sometimes it's the mustachioed villain tying the orphan onto the railroad tracks. We use rhythm, melody and harmony mostly to convey these sorts of things, but our best tool is orchestration. The noble trombones, the heroic trumpets, the sexy saxes; each instrument has its clichés. In addition to the choice of instrument, we can use different registers, mutes and techniques that can work against those clichés. Saxes trilling are not sexy. Trombones sliding are comical, not noble.

The brass at **H** is purposely voiced low. That register combined with the plungers creates grunting sounds. Until writing this paragraph, I never thought about why I wrote these grunts and what they convey in our story. So far, our protagonist has been suavely seducing the less experienced young woman. I think maybe Letter **H** represents the sex act itself, with the brass representing our guy grunting and the saxes offering faint resistance. She can't help herself and lets down her guard for a few moments, joining in the fun with those syncopated 5-part rhythmic voicings in the same register as the brass (**G10, H4** and **H8**).

The Climax

In **I1-2** the horns answer the vocal much as the bones did in **A1-3**, but much more forcefully. The brass are voiced in their most powerful register with the saxes supporting them in their powerful low register. The trumpets are voiced in upper structure triads and 7th chords (E♭/D♭7 and C#7/B). The extremely dissonant G (+11 on the D♭7) in the 3rd Trombone creates a -9 interval with the G# (enharmonic equivalent to the 5th of the D♭7) in the 1st Trombone. It then resolves chromatically down to the consonant F# (5th of the B7). The dissonance shifts from the bones up to the trumpets. Where do we go from here?

We are pushing to the climax.

The saxes make their last try at resistance with their long E13+11 voicing in their high register, before they relax into submission and join the brass on the *and* of 2 in **I4**. It's a 13+11 chord, but voiced lower. At the same time the brass play a rhythmic ascending chromatic scale in double octaves with the lead trumpet climaxing on a syncopated high E♭. This is the highest note in the entire chart, and comes at the peak moment—excuse the pun.

Smoking Cigarettes

The old sexual cliché of smoking a cigarette in bed after having sex may have gone the way of the horse and buggy—smoking is unhealthy, dirty, and foul-smelling, so maybe we need a new cliché—cuddling? I can live with that. Anyway, that's what happens in **I5-10**.

We return to the vocal/trombone call-and-response pattern of letter **A**, but now the bones are joined by the saxes for an extension with repeated melody and added measures and words using a chromatic bass line for the re-harmonization. Where once we were two people in conflict, we are now happily in agreement. The final peck gets a fall-off, leaving us with just the bass and drums, as if to say, "We don't need to talk." The ascending Jimmy Blanton bass cliché ends on the downbeat of **I10** and creates a break, leaving just enough time for Denzal to remind us of how this all started—our title, "Those lips, those eyes!"

Coda

It is now time to sum up the entire story and leave the audience with a clear picture of what just transpired. Unlike the codas in Beethoven symphonies that pound away tonic/dominant forever, we've got four measures to say it all. I want to celebrate with a strong ending. Denzal reaches up to a high D—the highest note he sings in the chart. As he holds out his victorious pitch, the band does my best version of a triumphal Beethoven coda.

The bass and trombones agree with Denzal on his tonic D, but then move down chromatically to the dominant (A) like the chord progression in the first two bars of our tune. In order to wind up on the A, we had to omit the C# in the descending scale and go directly to C natural. After they arrive at the dominant

(A) there is a short drum break to set up the final tonic chord.

While this is going on in the bones and rhythm section, the trumpets and saxes are voiced in 4-part close *tutti*. The lead trumpet, lead alto and bari are all doubled and alternate 5-1, 5-1, 5-1. Dominant/tonic—like Beethoven, except that the harmonies go along with the bones and bass. The inside parts create tension with the outer parts, giving us stability.

What does the coda have to do with this chart?

The trumpets and saxes are giving us one last shot at the rhythm and shape of our initial motif—dotted quarter/quarter. If you didn't get it the first time, they repeat it two more times. Had I used the minor 3rd interval from the motif, it would not have sounded final enough. 5-1 works so much better than 5-3. The rhythm and shape are enough for us to get the point.

After the drum break we get the cliché final tonic 13+11. I can think of hundreds of charts that end with this exact voicing. Why is it so satisfying here?

- Continuity—we have used the same upper structure voicing (E/D7) numerous times in the chart.

- The final lead trumpet note is higher than the previous phrase, but not as high as the climax in **I4**.

- The brass are voiced in their strongest register and are joined and supported by the saxes in their strong low register with the solid root, 5th, 3rd, 7th on the bottom.

- Last, but not least, the lead trumpet note (B) is our happy note (the 6th in the key of D) bringing a smile to our faces. We are in agreement: although our corny cliché line seemed like a long shot in the beginning, it worked to bring together two opposing entities (musically and symbolically). If only real life were this easy.

[Listen again to **9-1: Complete Arrangement** and see if all the elements add up. Is there sufficient drama? Do we feel satisfied at the end? Did everyone get an interesting and gratifying part to play, or do some of the musicians feel left out of all the fun? The musicians' enjoyment travels over the footlights and infects the audience. I love when audience members will come up to me after a set or concert and tell me, "It looks like you guys are having a great time." Well, yeah, we are. That's why we do it.]

Coda

Some thoughts about writing songs:

1. Keep it simple and direct.

2. Make the words and music singable and fun to pronounce.

3. Keep the singer's range in mind.

4. Honor the highest and lowest notes (where they fall in the trajectory of the song) and the important words.

5. Use your motif as much as possible. If you can't repeat it any more, sequence it. If you can't sequence it, develop it. The difference between great songwriters and everyone else isn't their motifs; it's how well they develop them.

6. Say the words and incorporate the rhythms and inflections of lyrics into the music. Don't accent the wrong syl-LA-ble.

7. Lyrics should rhyme to help us to understand the words, make it feel organized and limit the possibilities. Avoid near rhymes (assonance)—they are cheap and confusing.

8. Earn the clichés you use.

9. Composers: Give your lyricist time to get used to your music. Lyricists: Vice versa. Welcome suggestions for changes, but don't let yourself be bullied into making bad choices. And don't be a bully. Songwriting is a collaboration.

10. If you can't decide between two choices that both work, look for the better third choice.

11. The words and melody are of primary importance. Rhythm, harmony, and orchestration cannot save weak words or melodies.

Ron Sunshine performing with the David Berger Jazz Orchestra at the Rainbow Room, New York. Photo ©2015 by Diana Velazquez.

Here are some concepts that I keep in mind when writing vocal charts:

1. Honor the words. Let the music help tell the story. The story takes precedence over the music, but that doesn't excuse bad music.

2. Make sure we can hear the lyrics. Don't let the instruments cover the words. When you are mixing, make sure that the vocal is sufficiently loud so that someone who doesn't know the words will understand them.

3. Less is more. Do not upstage the singer.

4. The singer is the star and the focal point. Don't let him/her stand around with nothing to do. Instrumental interludes should generally be short.

5. Verses can be useful as introductions and interludes.

6. Modulations are more common in vocals than in instrumental charts, especially if the song is diatonic with simple chord changes.

7. Challenge the singer to be his/her best, but don't try to teach them. This goes double when working with established singers.

When it comes down to it, your job is to make the singer look and sound good. Do your best to give the band some fun stuff to play, but when there is a singer, the audience's primary relationship is with him/her. Create nice settings—find new ways to think of the songs—always look for the deeper meaning of the words and music while catering to the singer's strengths, weaknesses, and personality.

Above all, have fun and respect the work. Never look down on the singer or song. It's your job to make the music great, and more importantly, create a setting that will inspire the singer to be great. If you fall short, it's on you. Rise to the challenge. Find the fun in the music. It may be just on the surface or buried deep inside, but if you are skilled and persistent, you should be able to tell a compelling story for three minutes. It's not a symphony. As Al Cohn said to me lo those many years ago, "It's a *vocal* chart."

Ever onward and upward,

David Berger
January 2, 2019

Glossary

4-part close harmony (Also called *4-way close* or *block chords*): Voicings with four different pitches within the same octave, and containing a root, 3rd, 5th and 7th (or variations of those pitches).

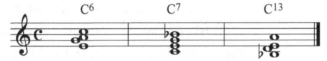

blue note: Notes from the blues scale that are approximately built on the ♭3, ♭5 and ♭7 of the home key. Jazz musicians will color these notes using bends and special intonation to evoke the feeling of the blues.

break: Within the context of an ongoing time feel, the rhythm section stops for one, two, four or even 8 bars. Most often a soloist will improvise during a break.

call-and-response: Back and forth, where both parts play the same same repeated figure, usually separated by an octave and played by different instruments, as in Sousa's *The Stars And Stripes Forever*.

Charleston: The following rhythm:

chalumeau register: Lowest octave-and-a-half of clarinet, below the break.

chart: Arrangement or orchestration.

chromatic: Moving by successive half steps. It can also mean non-diatonic.

coda: (Sometimes called the *outro*) A new section added to create a satisfying ending.

comp: To improvise accompaniment. Short for "accompany."

come sopra: As above.

concerto: Loosely, a piece that features a solo instrument. Traditionally concerti are three movements in length; the first movement being in sonata allegro form. Ellington's concerti (*Concerto For Cootie, Echoes Of Harlem, Boy Meets Horn*) are 1-movement sonata allegro forms, as is Strayhorn's *Charpoy*.

concerto grosso: A piece that features a small group of solo instruments within a larger ensemble. Ellington's *Jam-A-Ditty, Battle Of Swing* and *Launching Pad* are great examples.

constant structure: Transposing a voicing to follow the melody.

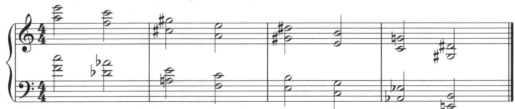

continuo: Improvised Baroque keyboard accompaniment that combines bass notes and chords.

contrary motion: Two or more voices moving in the opposite direction.

cross-sectional orchestration: Scoring for dissimilar instruments in unison or harmony, i.e. trumpet/tenor sax.

derby or hat: Metal mute for brass instruments in the shape of a derby. It may be fanned open and closed, or held still in front of the bell of the instrument, creating a distant sound.

diatonic chords: Those triads and 7th chords that occur naturally (with no accidentals) in major and minor keys. In jazz, although we use all seven chords and call them by number (*I, ii, iii,* etc), we normally only use the formal names for the tonic, dominant and subdominant (*I, IV* and *V*). Also in jazz, very often triads and 7th chords are interchangeable. The chord symbol "C" usually infers that we could add a 6th or a major 7th to the triad.

displaced rhythm: Starting a rhythm on a different beat or part of the beat.

dogfight: A back and forth quick call-and-response where both parts play the same repeated figure, usually separated by an octave and played by different instruments, as in Sousa's *The Stars And Stripes Forever.*

doit: An upward gliss (non-fingered portamento).

Drop 2: Semi-open voicings that are created by taking a 4-part close harmony and dropping the second voice from the top by one octave.

Drop 2 and 4: Semi-open voicings that are created by taking a 4-part close harmony and dropping the second and fourth voice from the top by one octave.

Drop 3: Semi-open voicings that are created by taking a 4-part close harmony and dropping the third voice from the top by one octave.

elision: Omitting the end of a phrase, so that the next phrase begins early.

fall-off: A downward non-fingered portamento. Fall-offs can be very short (also known as a Snooky Young fall-off—generally a half step), short (a 2nd or 3rd) or long (an octave or so. Trombones use their slides, trumpets the half valve, and reeds a downward fingered gliss. The Snooky Young fall-off is lipped down by the trumpets and reeds. The trombones use fast slide movement. Fall-offs are non-measured and left to the discretion of the player(s).

fills: Melodic, chordal or rhythmic answers.

functional chord substitution: Replacing harmonies with other harmonies that conform to the tradition of tonic/dominant pull. The use of secondary chords (*ii, iii* and *vi*), secondary and applied dominants and chords borrowed from the minor modes (♭*III*, ♭*VI* and ♭*VII*), and some temporary modulations are also included.

groove: The composite rhythm. Generally refers to combined repetitive rhythmic patterns in the rhythm section, but may also include the horns. Standard grooves may be notated by name (bossa nova, swing, ballad, etc.). Manufactured grooves will either combine elements of two or more grooves (i.e. drums play swing, while the bass plays a tango) or wholly new elements, which will need to be notated specifically.

head: Melody chorus.

hexatonic voicings: Generally a triad stacked on top of another triad. Two very useful varieties are a minor triad over another minor triad built a major 7th apart and augmented triads built a major 7th apart.

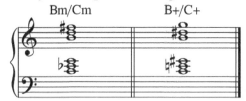

interlude: A contrasting form sandwiched between two chorus forms.

intro: Short for introduction.

inversion: Playing a motif upside down.

linearly derived harmonies: Harmonies that result from the confluence of melodic lines and don't conform to standard chord nomenclature.

mixed meter: regularly changing the meter signature or implying a superimposed meter.

modulation: Changing key. There are four basic types of modulation:

sequential: Repeating the last figure starting on a different pitch and continuing in the new key.

common tone: Holding over or repeating the last note from the old key to the new key.

dominant motion: Preceding the new key with its dominant.

modulation, continued:

    abrupt (sudden): No preparation.

motif: Short melodic and/or rhythmic fragment.

non-functional (color) harmonic substitution: Replacing harmonies with chords outside the key without preparation. This can include parallel harmonies, triads over non-related bass notes, etc.

oblique motion: One voice repeats a pitch or pitches while another voice or voices move in parallel and/or contrary motion.

octave displacement: Changing the octave of one or several notes in a phrase.

octave unison: Two or more instruments playing the same pitch or pitches but separated by an octave.

ostinato: A short melodic phrase repeated throughout a composition, sometimes slightly varied or transposed to a different pitch.

pad: Harmonized chordal background consisting mainly of notes of longer duration. It used to be called "organ background."

parallel motion: Two or more voices moving in the same direction.

passing chords (sandwich chords): Interjecting smooth harmonies to create interest and avoid static harmonies. There are four basic methods:

    diminished: Determine the anchor chords, voice them with the basic chord, and then build diminished chords on the in-between notes (see example next page).

chromatic (planing): If the melody moves by half step or half steps, determine the anchor chords, voice them with the basic chord, and then working backwards, move the underparts chromatically in the same direction as the melody.

dominant: Determine the anchor chords, voice them with the basic chord, and then working backwards, build dominant 7th chords a perfect 5th above the upcoming chord. Very often altered dominants and tritone substitutes are used.

diatonic: When the melody moves stepwise in the key of the chord change, determine the anchor chords, voice them with the basic chord, and then working backwards, move all the voices stepwise in the key in the same direction as the melody. This is the least used of the four approaches, so although it is simple and non-chromatic, it can sound fresh.

peashooters: Brass instruments with small bores. They create a brighter sound than the normal size horn.

pedal point: Sustaining or repeating a pitch while the other voices move. Using the dominant is the most common, but tonic pedal point is also used. Most often the pedal is voiced below the other parts, but it can also be on top (often called inverted pedal point) or in the middle.

pixie mute, plug: Originally called French straight mute or plug. A smaller version of the straight mute that fits in the bell of the horn beneath a plunger. A straight mute extends too far, and would prevent the plunger from covering the bell of the instrument.

plagal cadence: *IV I*, as in "Amen."

pyramid: Individual single note entrances that lay on top of the preceding entrances.

re-harmonization: Creating new harmonies to a previously existing melody. This can be a total re-vamping, isolated chords or something in between.

real sequence: Repeating a motif starting on a different pitch, and keeping all the intervals the same as the original. This results in stretching the tonality or leaving it altogether.

retrograde: Playing a motif backwards.

retrograde inversion: Playing a motif upside down and backwards.

ride pattern: The most common repetitive swing figure that drummers play on the ride cymbal. It can also be played on the crash cymbal or hi-hat.

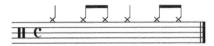

riff: Motif that gets repeated. Very often the harmonies change beneath it.

Schenkerian analysis: A method of musical analysis of tonal music based on the theories of Heinrich Schenker (1868–1935). The goal is to extract the underlying structure of a tonal work and to show how the surface of the piece relates to this structure. (from Wikipedia)

syncopation: Accenting the weak beat or weak part of the beat, while avoiding the following strong beat or strong part of the beat.

scronch: Accented quarter note on beat 4. It can be short or tied over into the next measure. Either way it gets the chord that belongs to the next beat.

sectional writing: Scoring for groups of like instruments, i.e. trumpets, saxes, etc.

serialization: The ordering of notes. Serial music limits the pitches to a specific set of intervals. Other elements can also be serialized, like rhythm, dynamics and orchestration. The goal is to create concise, integrated pieces. 12-tone music uses a row of all 12 chromatic pitches and serializes the intervals. Rows can and often do contain fewer notes (3, 4, 5, etc.).

shout chorus (also known as the *sock chorus*): The climax of the chart, where "everything comes together" and all the horns play.

slash chords: Generally triads over a related or non-related bass note. Sometimes triads or 7th chords over a different triad or 7th chord.

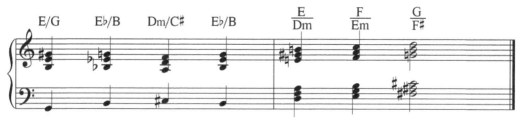

smear: Hitting a note flat and lipping up to the pitch. Alto saxophonist Johnny Hodges was legendary for this, but it is also used for expression on other horns and strings.

soli: A harmonized passage for two or more instruments playing the same rhythm.

song form: Generally 16, 32 or 12-bar forms (consisting of 4-bar or 8-bar phrases) that can be repeated and improvised on. The most common song forms in jazz nd the American Songbook are: *aaba, abac* (or *abab'*) or *aab* (the Blues).

song form notation: Lower case italicized letters represent phrases, i.e. *abcd*. Repeated letters mean that the material repeats verbatim or verbatim with a different turnaround, i.e. *aaba*. Letters with an apostrophe represent phrases that start the same, and then go somewhere else, i.e. *abab'*. Generally standard song phrases are 8 bars in length, but on rare occasions, they could be 4 bars, 6 bars, 10 bars, 16 bars, etc. Here are some examples of well-known songs with these forms:

abcd   *Stella By Starlight* (8-bar phrases)

aaba   *Honeysuckle Rose* (8-bar phrases)

aab   *The blues* (4-bar phrases)

abab'   *There Will Never Be Another You* (8-bar phrases)

abac   *Gone With The Wind* (8-bar phrases)

aaba+tag   *Moonlight In Vermont* (6-bar *a* sections, 8-bar bridge, 4-bar tag)

spread chords or chorale voicings: Open voicings that generally have the root on the bottom.

stop time: A regular pattern of short breaks, often filled in by a soloist. The melody chorus of *Sister Sadie* or the Harlem Globetrotters' version of *Sweet Georgia Brown* are famous examples.

stretto: The final section of a fugue, where the subjects occur in more rapid succession than previously, causing overlapping. The effect is to build tension, create a climax and ultimately lead to a feeling of finality.

subtone: Way of playing reed instruments very softly, usually in the lower register. The effect is that we hear more air than tone.

swing: The perfect confluence of rhythmic tension and relaxation in music, creating a feeling of euphoria. Characterized by accented weak beats (democratization of the beat) and eighth notes that are played on the first and third eighth notes of an eighth note triplet. Duke Ellington defined swing as when the music feels like it is getting faster, but it isn't.

tacet sheet: A part for an instrument that does not play a particular movement or piece. It has no notes, only the word TACET, and is used as a place saver.

symmetrical voicings: Generally 6- or 8-note voicings that, if divided in half, will contain all different pitches but the same intervals. The intervals can be in the same vertical order or inverted.

tag or tag ending: Derived from vaudeville endings. The two most common are ||: IV/IV⁰ I (second inversion) V/ii ii V :|| I and ||: iii V/ii ii V :|| I. Repeats are optional.

tertian harmony: Harmony built in thirds.

tessitura: The general range of a melody or voice part specifically; the part of the register in which most of the tones of a melody or voice part lie.

thickened line: Voicings that are constructed from the melody down, with everyone playing the same rhythm as the melody. These kinds of voicings generally omit the roots and are not concerned with inversions, since the bassist is stating the root progressions.

thumb line: A slow moving (half notes or slower) mostly stepwise unison or solo line used to accompany a melody. Thumb lines stay away from melody and bass notes, and mostly contain 3rds and 7ths.

tonal (or diatonic) sequence: Repeating a motif starting on another step of the scale, but not adding accidentals, so that you are still in the original key.

tritone interval: A diminished 5th or augmented 4th. This interval contains three whole steps.

tritone substitution: substituting a dominant 7th chord built a diminished 5th away from the original chord.

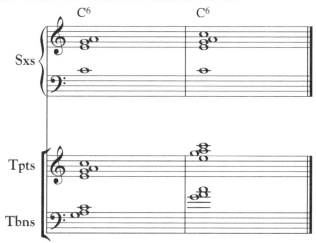

truncation: Shortening by lopping off the end of a motif, phrase, or passage.

turnaround: A series of chords that take us back smoothly to the first chord of a progression (usually the tonic). Although generally used to refer to the last two bars of an 8-bar phrase, *I vi ii V* and *iii vi ii V* are commonly called turnarounds wherever they occur.

tutti voicings: 4-part close ensemble voicings doubled throughout the brass and reeds. There are several variations, but the great majority fall into two categories: either the reeds double the trumpets in their register or an octave below. This is generally determined by the range of the lead trumpet. If he goes above the staff, the reeds are voiced an octave below.

unison: Two or more instruments playing the same pitch or pitches in the same octave.

upper structure triad: A non-related major or minor triad placed above a 7th chord.

vamp: A repeated 2- or 4-bar chord progression usually supporting riffs. Coming from vaudeville, vamps are often used for intros, codas and interludes (especially just before a singer enters).

voicing: The specific pitches, inversion, and spacing that make up a chord.

Index

About the Author

Jazz composer, arranger, and conductor David Berger is recognized internationally as a leading authority on the music of Duke Ellington and the Swing Era. Conductor and arranger for the Jazz at Lincoln Center Orchestra from its inception in 1988 through 1994, Berger has transcribed more than 1000 full scores of classic recordings, including more than 500 works by Duke Ellington and Billy Strayhorn. Several of these transcriptions, and a number of original arrangements, were featured in the 2013 Broadway hit, *After Midnight.*

In 1996 Berger collaborated with choreographer Donald Byrd to create and tour *Harlem Nutcracker*, a full-length two-hour dance piece that expands the Tchaikovsky/Ellington/ Strayhorn score into an American classic. The 15-piece band assembled to play this show has stayed together as the David Berger Jazz Orchestra, performing Berger's music in New York City and on tours throughout the United States and Europe.

Berger has written music for symphony orchestras, television, Broadway shows and films, and has composed and arranged for Duke Ellington, Jazz at Lincoln Center, Quincy Jones, and the WDR Big Band. He has also arranged for dozens of singers including Jon Hendricks, Betty Carter, Freda Payne, Natalie Cole, Rosemary Clooney, Madeleine Peyroux, Milt Grayson, Cécile McLorin Salvant, Susan Graham, Denzal Sinclaire, Champian Fulton, Freddie Cole, Jessye Norman, Kathleen Battle, and Kevin Mahogany.

Berger has taught jazz arranging and composition for 30 years in the New York City area at the Juilliard School, Manhattan School of Music, The New School, William Paterson University, Montclair State University and Long Island University. In addition to private teaching, Berger travels around the U.S. and Europe, performing clinics with high school and college jazz bands.

Residing in New York City, Berger currently composes and arranges in addition to writing a weekly blog about the juncture of art and life.

www.SuchSweetThunderMusic.com
www.DavidBergerJazz.com

Other Books by David Berger

- *Creative Jazz Composing & Arranging*
- *Life in D♭: A Jazz Journal*
- *High School Jazz: A Director's Guide to a Better Band*
- *Fancy Footwork: The Art of the Saxophone Soli*
- **COMING SOON:** With Chuck Israels:
  The Public Domain Song Anthology

CDs are available from **SuchSweetThunder.com**, **Amazon.com**, and **cdBaby.com**. Downloads can be purchased at those outlets as well. Downloads and streaming are available at all online digital outlets.

CDs by David Berger

- *Harlem Nutcracker* / David Berger & The Sultans of Swing
- *Doin' the Do* / David Berger & The Sultans of Swing
- *Marlowe* / David Berger & The Sultans of Swing
- *Hindustan* / David Berger & The Sultans of Swing
- *Champian* / Champian Fulton with
  David Berger & The Sultans Of Swing
- *I Had the Craziest Dream:
  The Music of Harry Warren* / David Berger Octet
- *Sing Me A Love Song: Harry Warren's
  Undiscovered Standards* / David Berger Jazz Orchestra
  with Freda Payne and Denzal Sinclaire
- *Old Is New* / David Berger Jazz Orchestra with
  Denzal Sinclaire (Download Only)

Available for download from **cdbaby.com**, **iTunes.com**, **allmusic. com**, **Amazon.com**, and **SuchSweetThunderMusic.com**. You can find many jazz arrangements, compositions and transcriptions at **SuchSweetThunderMusic.com**.

Book Reviews

Creative Jazz Composing & Arranging, Vol. I

David Berger shares the secrets of writing music that's fresh, original and memorable, distilled from a lifetime of composing and arranging for the iconic bands of Quincy Jones, Wynton Marsalis and the Jazz at Lincoln Center Orchestra. Downloadable complete scores and recordings are included.

"I love this book. The discussion of the musical content is clear and concise, while a respect and passion for the music and the creative process are evident throughout. The big band scores are brilliant— steeped in the rich tradition of jazz, but also conveying the unique musical character that is David Berger.

It is a joy to get inside the head of one of my favorite jazz writers and bandleaders."

Bill Dobbins
Professor of Jazz Composition and Arranging
Eastman School of Music

Life in D♭: A Jazz Journal

David Berger, renowned jazz composer, arranger, band leader and educator, tells you what it's like... from falling in love with jazz as a boy, to his first jobs as a musician and arranger... from international triumphs with the Jazz at Lincoln Center Orchestra, to heartbreak and success with his own Big Band. The chapter on transcribing alone is worth the price.

"David tells it like it is. A compelling read for every musician and music lover."

Quincy Jones
Producer/musician/composer/arranger

High School Jazz: A Director's Guide to a Better Band

The culmination of 40 years of teaching jazz, with proven techniques to help you bring a band to its highest potential.

"I have been a high school jazz band director for 21 years, and this is the best book I've ever seen about teaching jazz band. If you want your band to sound authentic and swing hard, study this book from cover to cover. Guaranteed to make your band better!"

Josh T. Murray
Jazz Band Director
Rio Americano High School, Sacramento

Creative Jazz Composing & Arranging, Vol. II: WRITING FOR SINGERS

"David Berger's new book *Writing for Singers* is a goldmine of valuable information on how to write and arrange music in a way that perfectly balances song, singer, and band. The insights in the opening pages, by Berger and lyricist Paul Mendenhall, convey a deep love and understanding of the Great American Songbook.

Berger has combined songs from the 1910s-1930s, with several of his originals (with lyrics by Mendenhall) in a variety of tempos, moods, harmonic schemes, and orchestrations for big band and vocalist. The music is superbly delivered by vocalist Denzal Sinclaire and David's big band.

Each chapter leads the reader clearly through the process of creating an arrangement from lead sheet to finished score. Each transposed score page includes a condensed C-score reduction at the bottom.

As in the first volume of this series, Berger's anecdotes of the professional jazz scene are insightful and entertaining. His description of the creative process, like his arrangements, reflects the gamut of the human experience with warmth and charm."

Bill Dobbins
Professor of Jazz Composition and Arranging
Eastman School of Music

"Dave Berger's *Writing For Singers* is as thorough a study of the craft and art of writing band arrangements for singers as I've seen, and it contains a wealth of information on the art of songwriting as well. There are beautifully performed and recorded examples (including exceptional performances by the fine singer, Denzal Sinclair), full scores, concert score reductions and extraordinarily detailed analyses of everything that went into the creation of these works.

Composers and arrangers develop habits of thinking and working that lurk partly below our consciousness, allowing us to write intuitively without slowing or stopping to intellectualize every decision. David is a particularly fast and intuitive writer/arranger. His songs and arrangements have taken him far less time to create than the analyses he presents here. He has meticulously dissected his ideas, described them in detail, traced their inspirations and assessed their effectiveness.

Little of this analytical activity surfaces when he's doing the musical work. It takes patience and profound attention to examine your own work and extract from it the things you might not have even realized you were thinking in its creation; all the things you think might be useful to someone learning the craft you have internalized. David has done this with thoroughness, clarity, and humor. It's hard for me to imagine anything important he's left out. This book is an invaluable resource."

Chuck Israels
Composer/arranger/bassist

Made in United States
Troutdale, OR
03/14/2024

18451261R00097